D1118955

Quotable
JIM MURRAY

Quotable
JIM MURRAY

THE LITERARY WIT, WISDOM, AND WONDER OF A
DISTINGUISHED AMERICAN SPORTS COLUMNIST

Linda McCoy-Murray

TowleHouse Publishing
Nashville, Tennessee

Copyright 2003 by Linda McCoy-Murray
All rights reserved. Written permission must be secured from the publisher to use or reproduce any part of this book, except for brief quotations in critical reviews or articles.

TowleHouse books are distributed by National Book Network (NBN), 4720 Boston Way, Lanham, Maryland 20706.

Library of Congress Cataloging-in-Publication Data

McCoy-Murray, Linda.
   Quotable Jim Murray : the literary wit, wisdom, and wonder of a distinguished American sports columnist / Linda McCoy-Murray.
      p. cm. -- (Potent quotables)
Includes bibliographical references.
   ISBN 1-931249-20-2 (alk. paper)
   1. Murray, Jim, 1920---Quotations. 2. Sportswriters--United
   States--Quotations. 3. Sports--United States--Quotations, maxims, etc.
   I. Title. II. Series.
   GV742.42.M87 M33 2003
   070.4'49796--dc21

                                                      2003000207

Cover design by Gore Studio, Inc.
Page design by Mike Towle
Cover photo provided by Linda McCoy-Murray

Printed in the United States of America
1 2 3 4 5 6 — 07 06 05 04 03

CONTENTS

FOREWORD

To CALL JIM MURRAY a writer is like calling Babe Ruth a ballplayer, the Grand Canyon a rock garden.

Jim Murray didn't see well for much of his life. His eyes often failed him, but his heart never did. And so he "saw" with his brain, his heart, and his soul. And he wrote what he saw.

He wrote with passion. He wrote with insight. He wrote about the soaring human spirit, and he wrote about the parade of lives most accomplished and flawed individuals.

And he wrote funny!!

I never thought of Jim Murray as a sportswriter. I always thought he was an observer of life who used sports as a vehicle; a prism from which he could measure and reflect character, integrity, honor, outrage, indignity, success, social ills, and, of course, humor.

Jim Murray was the funniest writer I've ever been around.

Sometimes the humor could make you smile softly; sometimes it was fall-down funny.

Sometimes it was the kind of funny that brought tears to your eyes . . . and not always because it was a belly laugh, but because the humor cut close to the core of our humanity . . . and you were moved by the humor!

That in and of itself was his most powerful and profound gift.

His humor was economical. It was light, and yet it was never without power or resourcefulness.

But the humor was the core of his writing. His humor was his sword—it deflated, it defrocked, and yet it never degraded!

How many times since his passing have I said to myself, or to anyone else in the room, "My God. Jim Murray would've had a great column on this!" And how many times I quietly regretted not having him around to get his opinion, his humor, and even his moral indignation.

We miss his talent. We miss his wisdom. And for anyone who ever was lucky enough to read his printed words—and there are tens of millions of us—we all miss his gigantic heart.

The truth is, nobody ever wrote better, or more eloquently, about anything for longer. And this is important, no one ever did it with a more self-effacing, pugnacious, yet graceful style, without self-celebration, than Jim Murray.

He was outrageous in his descriptive prose at times, but he never posed, he never postured.

Jim Murray was the most disproportionately humble man who ever rode his fingers across a Royal keyboard. He could've written from Mount Olympus, yet you never got the feeling that he ever felt he was anything more than a guy from down the block.

I don't say it about anybody I know anymore, and I'm sorry I can't.

He was better than the games themselves.

He wrote of the exalted, and he wrote of the broken shells of humanity.

He wrote about glory, and he wrote about dysfunction.

He wrote about men and women whose calling inspired us, and his words added to the inspiration.

Jim Murray wrote about the spirit in all of us, and about our own wretchedness, too!

He could make us proud, and he could shame us.

Jim loved sports, but he didn't write about just sports. He wrote about the things that matter most in life: commitment, courage, compassion, love, and truth. And everywhere he wrote, there was the laughter.

I miss having breakfast with Jim Murray's words. I know I speak for anyone who ever had the good fortune to open up a newspaper and read his daily offerings.

The good news is that Jim Murray's words live forever, and through them, so does he!!

So enjoy Jim's most memorable quips, asides, musings, observations, and his most articulate and thoughtful one-liners. They are some of this country's most beloved and original creations.

They tell us about him. They tell us . . . about us.

—Roy Firestone

ACKNOWLEDGMENTS

HELP IS ONE OF those four-letter words not often used. In this case, I found myself asking for a lifeline at every turn of the page, every paragraph, semi-colon, comma, and period. Over the course of nearly four decades, my late husband Jim Murray wrote an estimated total of ten thousand columns as a syndicated sports columnist for the *Los Angeles Times*, in addition to writing magazine articles and giving speeches.

As Dave Kindred of *The Sporting News* said, "Only Jim always got it right and always got it funny." Picking and choosing the quotes for this book was fun, yet extremely challenging, as it was indeed a smorgasbord. I'm certain many favorites were missed, which hopefully will prompt submissions from readers. There is always room for *Quotable Jim Murray*, Volumes II, III, IV, etc.

I want to acknowledge a handful of people who made it possible for me to meet my deadlines, which made my publisher and editor Mike Towle very happy. Mike, who truly idolized Jim Murray, is a master at publishing the *Potent Quotables*, and I thank my sportswriter friend John Reger from Orange County, California, for steering me to TowleHouse Publishing.

Without the daily emotional support from my longtime friend and confident Julia McGuire, editor and publisher of the *Hudson Valley Literary Magazine* in Cornwall, New York, my energy level would have been sucked down into the empty ink wells of time. And, thanks to my brother Bruce Carothers in Columbus, Indiana, who had encouraging e-mails waiting on my computer screen every morning, without fail. The ever-loving support of my son Bill McCoy kept me smiling with his great sense of humor, and he would never allow me to give up on the book project.

I wish to thank 2002 graduates Adam Karon and Ryan Pearson, UCLA and USC respectively, who, as Murray Scholars, gave unselfishly of their time to research and record many of the quotes. UCLA students Eli Karon and Sam Slomowitz also rolled up their sleeves to archive on weekends.

My staff and interns at McCoy-Murray Enterprises over the past two years were vital to the down-to-the-wire manuscript completion. In alphabetical order, I express my deepest appreciation to Julie Filkoff, Scott James, Alexandra Palmer, Shanassa Roen-Padilla, Jennifer Wills, and Erin Woods.

More help came from writers and editors I trusted with my life, which is very risky, so I'm told. My deepest trust was placed in the hands of Jim's "Pen Pal" and my friend Woody Woodburn, sports columnist for the *Daily Breeze* in Torrance, California. Woody's editing—beginning, middle, and end—saved me embarrassment, as well as saving reams of paper that never met my Fellowes shredder.

A sincere thank you to Roy Firestone, one of Jim's biggest cheerleaders, for writing the book's foreword and for providing unlimited support.

Last but not least, major kudos go to the Cecilia B. de Mille of photography, my friend Anita Bartlett, who caused Kodak stock to soar. Rolls and rolls of film were used as she tried to capture the "perfect portrait" for inside this jacket cover. For her talent and her patience, I extend my deepest appreciation. It's nice to know that drinking Lake Erie every day has helped maintain an aging skin, and she still made me look good while looking a bit nunish. (Read the introduction, and you'll understand.)

INTRODUCTION:
FOR THE
UNDYING RECORD

Basically, I find most people hate to be informed. . . . People need to be amused, shocked, titillated, or angered. But if you can amuse or shock or make them indignant enough, you can slip lots of information into your message. . . .

Satire is the best weapon in the writer's arsenal to attack injustice. Frothing at the mouth turns the reader off. Angry voices are always assaulting us from all sides. The humorless we always have with us. And they always have their soapbox. The din of indignation gets deafening.

—Jim Murray, from his 1993 autobiography

I N HIS OWN CONSTERNATION, Jim Murray prophesied that when he died, "Hell, I won't be out of here six months and they'll be saying, 'Jim Who?'"

Those words crossed my mind many times in the six months after his death, subsequently planting the seeds for the idea to establish the Jim Murray Memorial Foundation, which provides journalism scholarships nationwide. What better way to perpetuate the wit and wisdom of one of most renowned and

revered sports journalists ever? Jim Murray, the patriarch of young
journalists. Murray Scholars.

 Quotable Jim Murray. A sportswriter's *Bartlett's* for the undy-
ing record. Everyone has his/her favorite Jim Murray quote, stem-
ming from the Indianapolis 500, "Gentlemen start your coffins"
to proclaiming Arnold Palmer as ". . . the greatest long putter
who ever lived. . . . he attacked the game of golf like a cop bust-
ing a crap game."

 Jim's loyal readers couldn't wait to wake to Jim Murray
three or four times a week. I woke up to Jim Murray every morning. There were volumes of quotables that passed between us in
the last dozen years of our life together. For instance, as an
observer of human behavior, Jim often viewed my high energy
and constant involvement in projects with, using my maiden
name for emphasis, "My God, Miss Carothers, don't you ever put
it in the hangar?"

 Jim was honored at a black-tie dinner, where, from the
podium, he sweetly told the filled-to-capacity International
Ballroom at the Beverly Hilton Hotel: "Linda brought three little
words into my life . . . is Linda there?"

 Our social calendar was always filled, which prompted wonderful wardrobing quotes. Being a big fan of full-body coverage,
Jim would say to me, "Can't you wear something a little more
nunish?"

 My prodding Jim to drink more water only incited his "I've
never known anyone to drink as much water as you do. You drink
Lake Erie every day!"

During our 1992 visit to a Hindu shrine in Bali, a monkey attacked me. Of that experience, Jim wrote a very funny column saying "I thought for a moment he was going to carry her [Linda] up the Empire State Building, and I would have to call out fighter planes to get her back—but all he wanted was the bottle of water under her arm." For months after he called me Faye Wray. But then he also called me Luther Burbank the minute I put my hands in dirt. He was 24/7 with Murray-isms.

The most endearing personal quote came in a bowling column he penned four days after our long-awaited marriage in March 1997, noting, "We were both free agents—twelve and a half years—and came in well under the salary cap." In closing he wrote, "Jerry Reinsdorf thinks he pulled the coup of the year signing Albert Belle for the White Sox? Forgetaboutit! I signed the real pennant winner. The Unreal McCoy. I wish I could have invited you all to the wedding, but home plate at Dodger Stadium was busy."

On August 16, 1998, the sports and literary worlds lost a treasure, but Jim Murray's body of work will forever be heralded in the archives of time. He gave us an era of excellence in journalism, integrity, and humility. He may be gone, but not forgotten. And never will they say, "Jim Who?"

—*Linda McCoy-Murray*

AUTO RACING

"I'd never drive anything you had to climb in the windows to start up."

On the Indy 500:
Gentlemen, start your coffins.

It's not so much a sporting event as a deathwatch. They hold it, fittingly, on Memorial Day.

America's Earache.

I have never faced Sandy Koufax's fastball, Muhammad Ali's left jab, Larry Csonka's rhinoceros charge. I have never hunted the lion, rode the shark or walked a jet wing. But I have braved the terror in the corners of Indy. I braved their track. I'd like to see them on mine—the dreadful stretch from the Harbor to the Santa Monica at five o'clock at night with your glasses sweaty, your shocks worn—and two California highway patrolmen in you rearview mirror behind on their quotas.

If an auto race writer were covering the story of the *Titanic*, how would he handle it? Simple. His story would start: "The maiden voyage of the S.S. *Titanic* was 'marred' today when the luxury liner hit an iceberg and sank with all hands." Or, it might be "The S.S. *Titanic* broke all lap and qualifying records for the North Atlantic run Monday before a severely damaged front end forced it out of the race."

They've moved the Indianapolis 500, honest. I went looking for it yesterday but it's not here anymore. I couldn't find an Andretti, Unser, Fittipaldi, Rahal or Penske. The most venerable auto race in history, the most prestigious, has become minor league. It's like going to Yankee Stadium and seeing Elmira play Binghamton. Nuns in a chorus line. Burros in the Kentucky Derby. The Final Four tournament with a height limit. The U.S. Open for guys with a handicap of five and over. Wimbledon with a limit on serve velocity.

If they took the steering wheel out, I couldn't tell the front from the back of one of those Indy cars. I have no idea what a magneto is, and I'd never drive anything you had to climb in the windows to start up.

On Mario Andretti:
What makes Mario Andretti unique is that he's the only guy who ever won the American driving championship, the world championship, and Indianapolis. That's like winning the Cy Young Award and the Triple Crown award in baseball, like playing both ways in the Super Bowl. Throw in stock car racing, which Mario also excelled in, and you have a decathlon of motor racing.

At this back-tie affair feting Murray are, left to right, Al Michaels, James Garner, Mario Andretti, Danny Sullivan, Jim, Carroll Shelby, and Dan Gurney. (Photo by Paul Lester Photography)

On A. J. Foyt:

People just seem to get on his nerves. He wins the pole in the temper derby by twenty miles an hour. If they named a car after him, it would be the Volcano.

On Parnelli Jones:

He was, as one longtime associate put it, "a race driver's race driver." He was the last guy in the world you'd want to see in your rearview mirror with the race on the line and two laps to go.

On Rick Mears:

Rick Mears won the seventy-fifth Indianapolis 500 Sunday. In a Roger Penske car. And the earth is round and water's wet. Coal is black. Kansas is flat. And dog bites man. It's not exactly stop-the-press stuff. Rick Mears is to auto racing what the old Yankees used to be to baseball, Notre Dame to football.

On Richard Petty:
When you talk of great streaks in sports, you usually begin with Joe DiMaggio's fifty-six-game hitting streak or Lou Gehrig's 2,130-game consecutive-game playing streak, or Byron Nelson's nineteen tournament wins in a season. Richard Petty once won ten stock car races in a row and twenty-seven in a season.

⌐⌐

On Johnny Rutherford:
The thing about Indianapolis champion Johnny Rutherford is that if Hollywood wanted to make the story of his life, there'd be no need to send for Paul Newman. Rutherford is better looking.

⌐⌐

On Al Unser Jr.:
It is the fondest wish of most fathers that sons follow in their footsteps, take over the family business, maintain the tradition. . . . Legend has it Unsers don't come equipped with heart, lungs and bloodstreams like the rest of us. They have cylinders and fuel pumps, and they bleed petroleum. If you check an Unser, you find a tachometer. In a few more generations, they'll be born with tires.

⌐⌐

BASEBALL

"I like to look down on a field of green and white, a summertime land of Oz, a place to dream."

I'll tell you what. I wouldn't know a balk from a hole in the ground. Walt Alston used to draw me pictures, and I still didn't get it. The infield fly rule is about as simple as calligraphy. It might as well be a Japanese naval code.

Baseball is a game where a curve is an optical illusion, a screwball can be a pitch or a person, stealing is legal and you can spit anywhere you like except in the umpire's eye or on the ball.

The charm of baseball is that, dull as it may be on the field, it is endlessly fascinating as a rehash.

On whether baseball is a business:
If it isn't, General Motors is a sport.

Catching a fly ball, or hitting a curved one, is not all that difficult. It may rank in difficulty somewhere below juggling Indian clubs and above playing an ocarina.

Baseball is a game played by nine athletes on the field and twenty fast-buck artists in the front office.

On Hank Aaron:

He is to enjoy only. The way he plays it, baseball is an art, not a competition. He is grace in a gray flannel suit, a poem with a bat in its hands.

On Walter Alston:

The only guy in the game who could look Billy Graham in the eye without blushing, who would order corn on the cob in a Paris restaurant.

On Hank Bauer:

(He) has a face like a clenched fist.

On Yogi Berra:

Yogi was a catcher who was as chatty as a Bronx housewife behind the plate.

On Roberto Clemente:

Roberto didn't have the grace of Henry Aaron or the dash of Willie Mays, but if you put all the skills together and you had to play one of them at the same position, it would be hard to know which to bench.

Jim Murray interviews Roberto Clemente. (Tidings photo provided by Linda McCoy-Murray)

On Joe DiMaggio:
Joe DiMaggio played the game at least at a couple of levels
higher than the rest of baseball.

On Don Drysdale:
Don Drysdale is a peculiar case. With the hitters in this league
he could lose an election to Castro. They are sure, to a man,
that he is baseball's version of a gas chamber and that batting
against him is like playing catch with hand grenades—with the
pins out.

On Ford Frick:
Ford Frick isn't the worst commissioner of baseball in history
but he's in the photo. I make him no worse than place.

On Orel Hershiser:
Norman Rockwell would have loved Orel Hershiser. The
prevailing opinion is, he wasn't drafted, he just came walking
off a *Saturday Evening Post* cover one day with a pitcher's glove,
a cap two sizes too big, and a big balloon of bubble gum coming
out of his mouth.

On six-foot-seven Frank Howard:
You get the feeling he's not actually a man, just an unreasonable facsimile.

On Reggie Jackson:
Everything that went on before he stepped to center stage was prologue. It was an opera that all led to the appearance of the star. When the scene was set and the overture over, Reggie gave 'em goose bumps.

On Sandy Koufax:
In a game where the vocabulary runs to four-letter words and the vocal range registers from loud to hoarse, Sandy is articulate and soft-spoken. Where the musical tastes run to rock'n'roll or hillbilly gut-bucket, Sandy prefers Mendelssohn and Beethoven.

On Tommy Lasorda:

If you had a license from God to construct yourself a baseball manager, you would probably begin with one with a big belly and short legs that were slightly bowed or pebbled with lumps so that they looked like sacks of walnuts. You would want one who had his own syntax, a voice that sounded like an oncoming train in a tunnel. It'd have to be a nice part for Vincent Gardenia.

On Mickey Mantle:

Mickey Charles Mantle was born with one foot in the Hall of Fame.

On Willie Mays:

Willie Mays is so good the other players don't even resent him. . . . The only thing he can't do on a baseball field is fix the plumbing.

On Mark McGwire:

You have to be around six feet five, 250 pounds to keep hitting a five-ounce baseball into orbit with a forty-inch, thirty-five-ounce bat as October rolls around.

Jim Murray and slugger Mark McGwire. (Mitchell Haddas photo courtesy of Linda McCoy-Murray)

On Satchel Paige:
Satch was probably the greatest thrower of a baseball in history.
. . . He is a walking reproof to the game wherever he turns up.
It is hard to see how anyone in the Hall of Fame can avoid
wincing when they see him coming. I hope they have the
decency to hide their plaques.

On Branch Rickey:
He could recognize a great player from the window of a
moving train.

On Cal Ripken Jr.:
Baseball lineups used to be full of guys like Ripken and
Aaron—and Gehrig. There were Charley Gehringers. . . .
What?! You never heard of any of them? Of course, you didn't.
But you've heard of tantrum-throwing and racket-throwing
tennis brats, you've heard of guys who had to be bailed out to
be suited up. . . . They make good copy. But you can have
them. I'll take Cal Ripken.

On Brooks Robinson:

Brooks Robinson with a glove has been a more devastating force in baseball for twenty-one years than Henry Aaron with a bat.

On Frank Robinson:

You know something about Robinson when you know he has played in more World Series than any man in the game today—five in two leagues. This may tell you more about the man than the fact that he is the only player in history to win the MVP in both leagues.

On Jackie Robinson:

If they slammed the door of the Hall of Fame on HIM, he'd kick it in. He'd make it if he had to come in a spike-high slide and some of baseball's most hallowed custodians would have spike wounds from ankle to ear.

On Pete Rose:

Pete Rose played the game for twenty-four years with the little boy's zeal and wonder until, if you closed your eyes, you could picture him with his cap on sideways, knickers falling down to his ankles and dragging a taped ball and busted bat behind him, looking for all the world like something that fell off Norman Rockwell's easel.

On Nolan Ryan:

Nolan Ryan is more than an athletic marvel. He's a medical marvel. His glove should go to Cooperstown, but his arm should go to the Smithsonian.

On Vin Scully:

Scully is the world's best at filling the dull times by spinning anecdotes of the one-hundred-year lore of the game. He can make you forget you're watching a 13-3 game...and take you with him to a time and place where you are suddenly watching Babe Ruth steal home.

On Tom Seaver:

If you braced Tom Seaver in the locker room, you got an illustrated lecture on how many fingers you put on the fastball, how many seams you gripped for the slider and a detailed physiological description of the proper wrist snap for the outside curve.

On Duke Snider:

Duke Snider seems likely to figure in the early returns of his first eligible ballot for the Hall of Fame. Some of the "phenoms" who have been supposed to replace him over the years seem more likely to figure in the first waiver lists for Spokane and points north.

On Casey Stengel:

Casey Stengel is a white American male with a speech pattern that ranges somewhere between the sound a porpoise makes underwater and an Abyssinian rug merchant.

On Fernando Valenzuela:

He threw the kind of canny twisters only a guy who had spent a lifetime in the bush leagues could throw.

A couple of legendary wordsmiths—Jim Murray and Yogi Berra.
(Photo courtesy of Linda McCoy-Murray)

On baseball writers:
Baseball writers are at that awkward age. Too old for girls and too young for Lawrence Welk.

On the designated hitter:
I think it's time to come to a uniform decision on this indelicate matter. I mean, either a team is the home nine or it's the home ten.

On Little League Baseball:
(It's) a juvenile activity that makes delinquents out of adults.

On baseball's slow pace:
I don't know when we got in such a hurry that everything had to be speeded up like one of those early jerky silent movies. If you're in a hurry go to an airport.

On baseball uniforms:

There are certain things which should be immutable in nature. Bankers and prime ministers should have oak-paneled offices. Queens should wear big floppy hats to the races. Circus aerialists should wear pink tights. And, baseball players should wear baseball uniforms. And baseball uniforms should be like tuxedos—the same today as they were fifty, seventy, one hundred years ago.

On match-ups:

Baseball loves to talk of legendary match-ups—Koufax vs. Gibson, Ruth vs. Grove, the Ruth Yankees vs. the McGraw Giants. None was deadlier than Giamatti vs. Rose. Its ripple effect will be felt in the grand old game for years. Like World Wars, there were no clear winners. They should set it to music and put it on Broadway. I have the name for it—*The Miserables.*

On ballparks:

I like to look down on a field of green and white, a summertime land of Oz, a place to dream. I've never been unhappy in a ballpark.

BASKETBALL

"Perhaps Bob Cousy is more Boston Pops and Arthur Fiedler than Arturo Toscanini."

I wouldn't know a moving pick from a moving picture. And the differences between a "high post" and a "low post," I leave to the post office.

⌐

On referees:
You make almost as much as a senior truck driver, and you get to see your wife and family sometimes as much as twice a month in a season. It's a nice job if you have thick skin, poor hearing, and you like flying through blizzards, room service, old movies, and Holiday Inns. A spy has a better social life. The piano player in the bordello gets more respect.

⌐

On Kareem Abdul-Jabbar:
Well, Abdul-Jabbar showed up for work for twenty-five years, always on time, always in shape to play, always at the top of the key, the low post, wherever he was wanted.

⌐

On Red Auerbach:
He directed all his life drive to winning an annual professional basketball championship which is the athletic version of collecting letter openers.

⌐

On Charles Barkley's joining the Phoenix Suns:
Like John Wayne taking over a platoon of college boys in *Sands of Iwo Jima*, or a mollycoddled greenhorn in *Red River*, Barkley, like a tough top sergeant, cajoled, muscled, needled, kicked bottoms and bullied a franchise into becoming a gang of terrorists in short pants on the floor.

On Elgin Baylor:
Elgin Baylor is as unstoppable as a woman's tears.

On Larry Bird:
The problem now for all the wise guys of the NBA is going to be, how you gonna keep 'em down on the farm after they've seen L. B.? Do the scouts now have to fly into Terre Haute and rent a dog? Are there more basketball players under the harvest moon than there ever were under the neon? Or is the Bird in the hand just a needle in the haystack?

On Wilt Chamberlain:
He looked, in poor light, like an office building with
kneepads. Gulliver. Goliath. The-Creature-That-Ate-
Basketball. Fee-fi-fo-fum.

On Bob Cousy:
Perhaps Bob Cousy is more Boston Pops and Arthur Fiedler
than Arturo Toscanini, more comic strip than a candidate for
the Louvre, a rhyme not a poem.

On Julius "Dr. J" Erving:
It will be interesting to see if he can be seen by the naked eye. It
is said that the good doctor was not born, he sprang full-blown
when somebody rubbed his hand across a lamp. He disappears
back into the bottle every night. He has three or four arms,
depending on whom you talk to. His eyes can see 360 degrees in
any direction, including the one in the back of his head. His
arms are so long he has to be careful not to step on them.

On Walt Hazzard:
He's only about six-two. You couldn't even get a nosebleed jumping off him. He'd have to stand on a box to find out what color Wilt Chamberlain's eyes are. He would be out-reached by so many guys at a boarding-house dinner that he might end up with the piece with all the fat on it and have no butter for his potatoes. He doesn't even look like a basketball player till the whistle blows and even then sometimes you think the coach just sent him in with a play.

On Chick Hearn:
They don't pay Chick to be blase. They don't pay him to understand officiating that goes against the home five. Chick is paid to make pro basketball exciting. And he does this better than anybody in broadcasting, and always has.

On Earvin "Magic" Johnson:
Magic without a basketball is . . . an offense against nature.

On Michael Jordan:
You go to see Michael Jordan play basketball for the same reason you went to see Astaire dance, Olivier act, or the sun set over Canada. It's art. It should be painted, not photographed.

⌒

On Bob Lanier:
If Bob Lanier played football, he'd have to line up one yard behind the line of scrimmage or be offside. Rumor has it his shoes are off-loaded at the Detroit River docks by tug. It takes him twenty minutes to unlace them. Even in basketball, he can get a three-second violation while standing on the sidelines.

⌒

On Shaquille O'Neal:
At seven feet one, 303 pounds, he looks as if he should have chairlifts running down the side of him. O'Neal is more than a building, he's a skyline.

⌒

On Pat Riley:
His hair is slicked back and oiled in the style that hasn't been popular since Rudolph Valentino's time. He is an educated man. He was a [journeyman] player himself, but his conversation is not peppered with the vulgarisms of the locker room.

On Bill Russell:
Bill Russell is a great defensive player, but what he does under the basket is as hard to see as Texas chiggers—as Bill intends.

On Bill Walton:
"Hello, I'm Bill Walton of the Boston Celtics." . . . As if there were another six-foot-eleven-inch redhead with size-fifteen tennis shoes and three-foot arms and the long, loose limbs of a basketball player at large on the grounds of the La Costa Hotel and Spa.

On Jerry West:

He has the quickest hands and feet ever seen on a guy without a police record. If they put a cap on him sideways and turned him loose on the streets of London, there wouldn't be a wallet in town by nightfall. . . . His nose has been broken so many times, he sneezes through his ears. Cigarette smoke would come out of his nostrils in corkscrew patterns. His septum is so deviated, he's breathing *yesterday's* air. He goes through life with such a *s-w-o-o-s-h* that there are only a few people certain what color he is.

On John Wooden:

Don't bang the drums slowly. Don't muffle the caissons, or lead a riderless horse. Strike up the band. Let the trumpets roll. Never mind the twenty-one-gun salute, just bring a plate of fudge. Raise your glasses in a toast if you must—but fill them with malted milk. John Wooden is not going out as a great general or field leader. This is not Old Blood and Guts or Old Hickory, this is Mr. Chips saying good-bye.

BOXING

"Boxing dirties almost everybody who goes into it. It's hardly ecclesiastic."

On Muhammad Ali:
He can be the Killer of Kinshasa against a George Foreman, but against the Lion of Flanders he's Henny Youngman.

On Butterbean:
I found myself dining with a round, hairless, surprisingly gentle man who looked like the bad guy out of a James Bond movie or the guard at the gangster's hide-out cabin. He was so white you could read by him. He looks about as athletic as a monk. In fact, he speaks in the soft tones of a priest hearing confessions.

On Oscar De La Hoya:
Oscar De La Hoya is too good to be true. I mean, he's more priest than pug, more altar boy than homeboy.

On Roberto Duran:
Rumor had it they found Duran in a tree, crouched on a limb with his ears laid back about to pounce on a passing deer. You shouldn't fight Roberto Duran, you should hunt him. When he came into a clearing, leopards scattered. Your best weapon in a fight with him is flight. Buzzards circle when he climbs into a ring.

On Aileen Eaton, fight promoter:
Boxing dirties almost everybody who goes into it. It's hardly ecclesiastic. It has yet to lay a glove on Aileen. Even Aileen's sister carefully skirts the problem that the skeleton in the family closet is wearing boxing gloves. Aileen comes of a very proper Vancouver, British Columbia, family and if you think the poor woman who had to explain, "My son, the folk singer," had troubles, think of Aileen's mother explaining, "My daughter, the fight promoter."

On George Foreman:
George Foreman was an absolutely awesome specimen. He could stun a buffalo with either hand, was as indestructible as an oak. George could kill anything that didn't move. But Sadler had to persuade him that fighters sometimes duck. In fact, when Dick held a heavy bag for George in gym workouts, cynics said it was because he was afraid George would miss it if it swayed on its chain.

On Don King:
With his electric hair and long-running monologues delivered in the booming bombast of Moses addressing the children of Israel, King feels he is the apotheosis of the breed.

On Scott LeDoux:

On his good nights, his face looks like a relief map of a flood — or a sunset over the Red Sea. His face has more stitches than a hook rug. He needs a sewing machine after a fight. Scott should always go into the ring with a picture of what his face looked like before he began stopping left jabs to the eyes; so the doctors will know where to put what when the fight is over. I swear, I don't know what a guy that clumsy is doing in a sport where you bleed. It's like getting into an Indianapolis car drunk.

On Sugar Ray Leonard, December 14, 1986:

At a recent press conference, the box-fighter Sugar Ray Leonard, proclaiming himself fed up with the sameness of the media exchanges, decided he would make up his own questions and give the answers he saw fit. Fair enough. I would, accordingly, be obliged if he afforded us the same courtesy. In our case, we would like the liberty of being able to make up the answers, however.

> *Question:* Sugar Ray, how can it be you're going to be coming back to fighting after a layoff since May 1984, after having only one fight in sixty months—that's five years?
>
> *Answer:* How does 30 percent of $47 million grab you?

On Sonny Liston:

His chest, neck, fist, thighs, wrist and calf are all one to four inches bigger than Patterson's. If you saw his footprint in the snow in the Himalayas, four expeditions would be launched to capture him. As long as he lives, man can believe in the Abominable Snowman.

On Joe Louis:

I have always thought Joe Louis the most honest athlete in the history of any sport. His phrases had the simple, uncomplicated sincerity of the child who sees no need to lie or the adult who sees no fear to make him want to.

On Archie Moore:

The early rounds of a Moore fight always remind me of a guy opening the hood of an engine and exploring around inside for weak spots. Only, when he finds them, he doesn't repair them. He makes them worse. It's a trick a lot of mechanics have, but with Dr. Moore, it's a high art. A loose bolt here, a sticky valve there, and by the time Arch has gotten through tinkering, the transmission falls out.

On Floyd Patterson:
The most destructible of fighters in the ring, he's the most indestructible out of it. . . . He's like the stagehand who keeps wandering through the set. He's Charlie Chaplin being chased by history, which keeps missing him.

On Jerry Quarry:
If Jerry Quarry's life story is ever made into a book, the title will be *Oops!*

On Sugar Ray Robinson:
Sugar Ray Robinson went through life like syrup over a waffle. The world looked to him like a two-pound palooka with a glass chin.

On Mike Tyson:
Prison is supposed to be about rehabilitation. There are social scientists who think you could put a man-eating shark in prison for a year or two and, with "help" (buzzword for therapy), he will come out a goldfish.

En route to the world heavyweight championship fight in Africa between Ali and Foreman in September 1974:

All right, my good man, hand me my jodhpurs and pith helmet and polish my monocle. Get the elephant ready. Fire up the African Queen. Phone Berlitz and see what they have in the way of Swahili. Get Tarzan and Jane on the drum and see what they're doing Tuesday. See what you can find out about the tsetse fly. Call me Bwana. Let's hope Grace Kelly and Ava Gardner get to fight over me in the steaming jungle night.

On boxers, in general:

He has to punch his way out of the ghetto. No one's going to send him to Yale and make him a stockbroker. He's willing to trade a detached retina or conversing in a hoarse whisper the rest of his life for the pink Cadillac, the penthouse, the wall-to-wall stereo system, the perks of pugilism. The only way he'll ever make brain surgery is on the table, not via medical school.

On Mike Tyson's fine for biting Evander Holyfield:

That may be the most expensive dining out in history.

FOOTBALL

"The Oakland Raiders are football's version of the Dirty Dozen. It's not a team, it's a gang."

Pro Football

On Lyle Alzado:
He found out what everyone finds out in Tinseltown sooner or later: You're only as good as your last picture. Or your last tackle.

On offensive lineman Bill Bain, who played for six NFL teams:
Once, when an official dropped a flag and penalized the Rams for having twelve men on the field, two of them were Bain.

On Fred Biletnikoff:
Fred Biletnikoff kind of looks like a troll. Or like something that arrived at the game by swan. He's got a name longer than the Warsaw telephone directory and a reach even longer. He can run just faster than he can walk but he's harder to keep track of than a mosquito in a dark bedroom. Sometimes, he seems to have arrived by parachute.

On Terry Bradshaw:

He always gave the impression he had just ridden into town on a wagon and two mules. He giggled. He was a country as grits, red-eye gravy and biscuits. He was as hyperactive as a puppy with a carpet slipper.

On Paul Brown:

A man of glacial contempt, spare and fussy, he treated his players as if he had bought them at auction with a ring in their noses and was trying not to notice they smelled bad.

On Dick Butkus:

What makes Butkus so valuable is, he often catches a football before it is thrown. This is because, in addition to catching footballs, he also catches people who have them. He shakes them upside-down till they let go.

On Don Coryell:
I have seen guys look happier throwing up.

On Conrad Dobler:
To say Dobler "plays" football is like saying the Gestapo "played" Twenty Questions. It's like being in a pup tent with a grizzly.

On John Elway:
He could write his name with a football, make it sing "Dixie," or open a bottle with one at twenty paces. He completed more passes than the Fifth Fleet on leave.

On Mike Garrett:
He eats more dirt than a gopher. His throat has the fingerprints of every linebacker in the league on it.

On Bob Hayes:
The only thing in the world that could ever keep up with him was trouble. Trouble runs an 8.6 hundred.

On Deacon Jones:
Deacon Jones is, quite simply, 20 percent of the Ram defense.
Just to equalize him requires 2.2 players.

On Chuck Knox:
A press conference was called yesterday to announce the new
head coach of the Rams. A limo pulled up, the passenger door
was opened, and nobody got out.

On Jack Lambert:
The first time you see Jack Lambert, you're tempted to ask what
he did with the fangs. Is that really tomato juice he's drinking or
something he bit out of the neck of Earl Campbell? Was his
coffin comfortable last night and what time does he turn into a
wolf? The pro from Pittsburgh, Transylvania. If hair starts
growing out of his face, get a mirror. Or get out. All middle
linebackers are a little crazy, but Jack Lambert is the Dracula of
the lot. Bela Lugosi gets the part. Karloff in cleats. Lambert
didn't come out of a college; he escaped from the laboratory.

On Bobby Layne:

Bobby didn't miss much in life. Wherever there was a drink to be drunk, a dance to be hooted, a song to be sung, a crap shoot to fade, a horse to be bet, a card to be dealt, Bobby sat in. . . . For Bobby, life was all fast Layne.

On Vince Lombardi:

Vince Lombardi looks as if he should be climbing down from behind the wheel of a six-wheeled semi and saying, "Okay, lady, where do you want the piano?"

On Dan Marino:

You're supposed to grasp the ball with two hands, hoist it behind your ear, wind up, plant your feet, close your eyes and heave. Marino just kind of flicks it fifty-five yards like a guy flicking lint off his tie.

On Joe Montana:

Giving Joe Montana the ball is like giving Rembrandt a brush or Hemingway a pen.

On Joe Namath:

In the little world of sports, there are words and incidents that come ringing down the corridors of time. There is Ruth calling his shot, Louis summing up an opponent with "He can run, but he can't hide," . . . and there is Joe Namath on the eve of the 1969 Super Bowl saying, "I guarantee it!"

On Merlin Olsen:

Merlin Olsen went swimming in Loch Ness—and the monster got out.

On nose guard Bill Pickel:

Putting a Rutgers man alongside Lyle Alzado would seem to smack of putting a nun in the Mafia.

On Jerry Rice:

Jerry Rice, like secondhand smoke, germ warfare and insider trading, should be banned. At least, this is the view of the NFL defensive backs. He should carry a Surgeon General's warning on his helmet.

On Pete Rozelle:

The Super Bowl is his monument. . . . Michelangelo has his *David*, Da Vinci his *Mona Lisa*—Rozelle has the Super Bowl.

On Lynn Swann:

Watching Lynn Swann catch a football is like reading Browning for the first time, or Byron. There's a purity to it that transcends the violence.

On Fran Tarkenton:

Tarkenton also says that his scrambles were actually artful geometric patterns. They looked on paper like a chart of a Rube Goldberg invention: Player A takes ball to Point B where he bumps into Defensive End C and reverses his field to Point D where water is dropped into hole which makes Linebacker E slip and allows Player A to duck under arm (F) and release ball (G) into air where it skids off helmet (H) of Cornerback I into waiting arms of Tight End J, who falls over Safety K into end zone for touchdown.

On Norm Van Brocklin:

A guy with the nice, even disposition of a top sergeant whose shoes are too tight.

On Billy Wade:

I'm glad the Rams traded Billy Wade. I won't say Billy was clumsy, but on the way back from the line of scrimmage with the ball, he bumped into more people than a New York pickpocket.

On Bill Walsh:

You half expect his headset is playing Mozart.

On Marc Wilson:

No one adds more suspense to a game than Wilson. He is one of the great mountains of indecision in the world of sport today. You watch Marc Wilson play football, and you wonder how he gets himself dressed in the morning. You'd think if you handed him a menu, he'd starve to death.

On Jack Youngblood:

If I were an NFL quarterback, whenever Rams defensive end Jack Youngblood begins thumping his right foot on the ground before the snap of the ball, I would call time and send out a cape and a sword and light a candle in the dressing room or make a call to my priest.

On Nebraska running back Lawrence Phillips's beating of his former girlfriend, and Coach Tom Osborne's support of Phillips:
Getting a 4:00 A.M. call that one of your star players has just dragged a woman down three flights of stairs by the hair is like the head of Ford Motor Company being awakened to be told the assembly line has just broken down.

On fans:
A Ram fan was said to be a guy who got his season tickets in February and his wife's Christmas present on Christmas Eve.

On interior linemen:
The interior line must be where guys on the lam from the police hide out. They're as anonymous as telephone operators.

On football coaches, in general:
In football, I could never figure out why every game had to start with a run off tackle, particularly when it always lost two yards or made no gain. But coaches look at me pityingly when I ask why. And give me an answer studded with obscure definitions of defenses that make me feel as if I asked Einstein to explain the expanding universe.

On the Raiders:
To hear the rest of the league tell it, the Oakland Raiders are football's version of the Dirty Dozen. It's not a team, it's a gang. It's not a franchise, it's a conspiracy. It wasn't recruited, it was captured. It's not the Oakland Raiders, it's Quantrill's.

On the Super Bowl:
The score belongs to the society pages. To preserve the spirit of the occasion, the teams should have played in tuxes or swallowtail coats and corsages. It's not an athletic event anymore, it's a carnival. Mardi Gras with first downs.

COLLEGE FOOTBALL

On Bear Bryant:
The man has been a refugee from a steam iron for forty years.

On Woody Hayes:
Hayes's success is no secret. He leaves no coal mine unturned in his search for players. He goes after great players like a playboy after chorus girls.

Woody was consistent. Graceless in victory and graceless in defeat.

On Joe Paterno:
He looks more like a nuclear spy than a football coach.

On Bo Schembechler:
What the iceberg was to the *Titanic*, what Little Big Horn was to Custer, Waterloo to Napoleon, Tunney to Dempsey, the Rose Bowl is to Bo Schembechler.

On Bud Wilkinson:
Bud Wilkinson doesn't look like your basic native American football coach. No broken nose. No limp when the weather turns bad. No shrieking tantrums from the top of the practice-field football tower. He doesn't look as if he'd ever punch a kid in the helmet, jerk on his facemask, or teach him to use an arm cast to break teeth.

On recruiting:

There is a certain number of players each year considered "blue chip" by the profession. The competition for these is lively and illegal. They used to tell a story of the recruit who ran afoul of the law and a faculty advisor protested, "But Coach! This guy robbed four banks and scored a seven on the college boards!" And the coach sighs and says, "I know! I know! But he runs the 40 in 4.3!"

I have nightmares thinking what might have happened if Edison could catch a football in a crowd, or the Wright Brothers spent their nights inventing the single wing. What if Louis Pasteur were a place-kicker?

Coaches spend fortunes cataloging the habits of opponents because football teams, like whooping cranes or spawning salmon and other migratory creatures like the Pacific gray whale, do the same thing in the same way over and over again, generation after generation. All teams, for example, run off tackle on first down, pass on third down, and punt on fourth. And whales mate in Magdelena Bay or Scammons Lagoon. And birds go south in the winter. And moss grows on the north side of trees.

"It's not a sport, it's bondage. An obses-sion. A boulevard of broken dreams."

The (golf) club has a natural instinct for trouble. It's a born outlaw. If it were human, it'd be robbing banks.

I don't know whether you know it or not, but a golfer on the scent of new clubs makes Don Juan look like a dependable, nine-to-five type, the marrying kind. A golfer looking for new clubs is like Joe Namath on a pickup. He'll dance with every girl at the prom.

I always wanted to have people point me out as I tee it up somewhere and have them whisper, "That's Jim Murray. You know, he holds the course record at L.A. North. Shot a 56. In the rain." I know, of course, I could never hold the course record at Riviera. The best I've ever done there is 103. Still, it's nice to dream.

When you get in the hole, and mark your score, you say, "I had five there." Then you look around, and if no one is looking at you funny, you frown and start to erase saying, "No, that's not right, it was only a four." This is known in golf as improving your lie. In other words, the first score was a lie, but the second was a better one.

When it comes to golf, I root for the course. In rodeos I root for the bulls. I'm a big fan of double bogeys. I love it when the weather at Pebble Beach is blowing a force ten gale and the flags are bent horizontal in the wind. I love unputtable greens.

It's not a sport, it's bondage. An obsession. A boulevard of broken dreams. It plays with men.

You know, golf isn't a talent. It's a trick. Just like writing a column.

I have a friend who calls golf "the pursuit of infinity." And I'll drink to that. It is a game that leaves the best of them. I have seen Ben Hogan shoot an 83. Around a clubhouse they'll tell you even God has to practice his putting. "In fact," goes the old joke, "even Nicklaus does."

Golf is a game where a "late hit" means a slice, not a fracture. It's where "rough" does not refer to Mean Joe Greene but high grass. Where hardly anybody ever needs crutches and the bleeding is all internal. The game is played at a walk and the most terrifying thing a golfer ever sees is a downhill putt. He doesn't need twenty yards of plastic to protect his rib cage, or a mouthpiece or face cage. No one has ever seen a golfer carried off the field. No neurosurgeons are needed at ringside. The turf is not artificial and hard as a throw rug on a boulder.

On Amy Alcott:
Amy Alcott was born to play golf as her idol, Katherine Hepburn, was to make movies. At an age when other little girls were trying on their mother's clothes and trying on lipstick and flowered hats and high heels, Amy was trying on size-4 cleats and windbreakers and hitting plastic balls into trash barrels in the family backyard in West Los Angeles.

On Tommy Bolt:

The press called him "Thunder." It fits his last name. It also fit his disposition. He was Golf's Vesuvius. Six feet of molten lava waiting to erupt. . . . but Bolt mad is a better golf show than most people happy.

On Ben Crenshaw:

Ben Crenshaw has the biggest feet, the babiest face and the longest swing ever seen on a golfer five feet nine inches tall. He looks like he should be just learning to ride two-wheelers, not win golf tournaments. For the rest of golf, it's a little like getting shot at from a baby carriage.

On Laura Davies:

Watching Laura Davies hit a golf ball is like watching Dempsey throw a right, Sampras serve an ace, Ruth put a three-and-two count into the seats or Jordan drop a three-point basket. You get goose bumps. The ball orbits. Nobody since Nicklaus has hit a ball so much higher, farther than the competition. The only words Davies needs on a fairway are, "I believe it's you."

Golfer Tommy Bolt, Linda McCoy-Murray, and Jim Murray. (Photo courtesy of Linda McCoy-Murray)

On Ben Hogan:

You see, I'm assuming Hogan's there, and I have this fantasy in which God is waiting for him and he says "Ben! We've been waiting for you!" and he shows him the course, which looks suspiciously like Riviera in 1948, and the Lord says, "Look! Hogan's Alley!"

On Bob Hope:

The really great sports passion of Bob Hope's life is golf. I don't suppose anybody alive has ever done more for the game, not Arnold Palmer, Jack Nicklaus, Lee Trevino, Ben Hogan, Gene Sarazen, not anybody, except possibly the Scotsman who invented it in the first place.

On Jack Nicklaus:

You always want Jack Nicklaus to win golf tournaments. The way you always want Ruth to get homers, Rose to get hits, Dempsey to get knockouts, Koufax strikeouts, and Mays fly balls at the fence.

On Greg Norman:

Golf's Job was a sight to behold on a fairway. The shock of cotton hair, the flashing blue eyes, out-thrust jaw, he was a combination Fearless Fosdick and Frank Merriwell.

On Ayako Okamoto:
You look at the numbers and you picture a truck driver or
sumo-sized striker of the ball. You look at Okamoto and you
want to ask, "Don't they make geisha girls anymore?"

On Arnold Palmer:
His rounds were never elegant exhibitions of stylish golf. They
were more like Dempsey-Firpo. Arnold and the course went
after each other like sluggers in dark rooms.

On Nick Price:
The Nick-Who-Is-Price has always had a healthy respect for
overwork. He respects it so much he avoids it. He treats golf as
a game, not a sentence. While not exactly happy-go-lucky, he
has been known to smile at a missed putt.

On Patty Sheehan:
When Sheehan came up to the same hall of horrors and faced
a 120-footer to two-putt and win the tournament, she knew
the drill. "C'mon, let's pull ourselves together, you can do it,"
she whispered to her ball. The golf ball, like all of us, responds
to a little flattery and a little tender encouragement, and it
purred right into the hole. She didn't say, "Don't go left, you
dog!" She pleaded with it. And it did as it was told.

On Charlie Sifford:
Golf was not a game for the ghettos. Neither did it leave any time for carrying picket signs, joining demonstrations, or running for office. Charlie birdied, not talked, his way through society prejudice.

On Sam Snead and Ben Hogan:
Sam Snead once said the only thing he feared on a golf course was lightning—and Ben Hogan.

On Sam Snead:
They never got Sam out of the hills—or the hills out of Sam. He'd still rather hunt squirrels than tour Europe. He came to Hollywood periodically but it didn't take. Sam made the film, and then went home to soak his feet, and then back to Virginia to shoot ducks. His pleasures are biblical and simple. Once, when he went to a nightclub, he ordered soft drinks all night— then took the bottles home in his pocket to claim the deposit.

Jim Murray and Sam Snead.
(File photo courtesy of Linda McCoy-Murray)

On Muffin Spencer-Devlin:

A golf green would seem to be the worst place in the world for anyone who has an uncertain psyche. You're always a putt away from a straitjacket. You don't play the game, you serve it. Yet, Muffin Spencer-Devlin says, simply, "Golf saved my life." She found, of all things, a serenity of purpose. For most players, golf is about as serene as a night in Dracula's castle. But for Muffin, it has a stabilizing effect.

On Craig Stadler and Tommy Bolt:

You think Craig Stadler is famous for apoplectic rages on the golf courses? He was Rebecca of Sunnybrook Farm compared to Bolt. Tommy practically invented club-throwing.

On Tom Watson:

Once upon a time there was this young golf player who looked as if he had just arrived by raft from the Mississippi River. He had this red hair and freckled face and a gap-toothed smile that made him look as if he had just stepped out of the pages of Mark Twain.

On Tiger Woods:
Golf is now a five-letter word. It's spelled "W-O-O-D-S."

On Mickey Wright:
The touring women pros contest for a mere $300,000 a year vs. $2 million the men shoot at. But there are fewer of them. Mickey Wright does Right Well, thank you, and, while she couldn't get in a poker game with Arnold Palmer, she could probably scare a Dow Finsterwald out of three of four pots.

On Babe Didrikson Zaharias:
She was America's tomboy, a hoyden in high heels, freckle-faced, gum-cracking. You were sure if she emptied her pockets, even when she was being presented at court, they would have a live lizard, a slingshot, a sack of marbles and some sticky licorice in them.

On the LPGA's lofty Hall of Fame requirements:
Mother never said it would be easy. Let the men admit wimps if they want. A woman's place may be in the Hall. But she'll have to crawl through barbed wire and shellfire and rocks before they'll let her in.

On Pebble Beach:
Pebble is a pirate which lies in wait for merchantmen in the most treacherous landfall this side of the Dry Tortugas."

On the Masters Tournament:
No one knows quite how the Masters golf tournament became a "major." The little world of golf looked up one morning and there it was on the doorstep marked, "Important. Refrigerate After Opening. Store With the British Open, the American Open, and PGA. Keep out of reach of children."

On St. Andrews:
You kind of get the bends when you walk on St. Andrews if you're a golfer. It's like a Catholic entering the Vatican for the first time, a Muslim reaching Mecca.

HOCKEY

"Hockey is the Bloody Mary of sports."

On Wayne Gretzky:
Gretzky will fill the seats. If he can fill the nets, too, he'll be the biggest bargain since Babe Ruth. The game needs glamour more than goals. He's already pulled the hat trick. He's put hockey on Page One. In Los Angeles. In August.

On Gordie Howe:
You ask a Canadian about Gordie Howe and the first thing he does is take his hat off and place it carefully over his heart. His eyes film up, this lump comes to his throat, and you get the eerie feeling that Citizen Howe is at least one of the twelve apostles. He wasn't born, he was found in the bulrushes.

On Bobby Orr:
You listen to old-time hockey people and you get the idea Robert Gordon Orr was born with skates for feet and a hockey stick for a right arm.

On Luc Robitaille:

If he played in Montreal, he would be on billboards and giving interviews in his native French. In L.A., they find out he's a hockey player and they ask him if he knows Gretzky personally, or they pronounce his name "Robo-telly" instead of the correct "Robo-tye."

Seeing a goal scored in hockey is like picking your mother out of a crowd shot at the Super Bowl.

Hockey is the Bloody Mary of sports.

There are two ways to play hockey: you can knock the puck off the player—or you can knock the player off the puck.

A puck, of course, is just a giant tiddlywink. It is designed for stealth, just one inch high, three inches across, and the color of skate shoes. The game is almost incomprehensible on TV, like a fox hunt on skates, in that you can't see the quarry.

HORSE RACING

*"Riding a racehorse is a little like
playing a grand piano. You've got to
have the touch of a concert artist."*

I've been covering horse races for twenty-five years and I still can't tell a colt from a filly except under very special circumstances.

A racetrack crowd comprises the greatest floating fund of misinformation this side of the pages of *Pravda*, the last virgin stand of optimism in our century.

On Affirmed, the 1978 Kentucky Derby winner:
Affirmed was the Star. A golden glow of a colt. A matinee idol. If he were human, he'd be Robert Redford.

On Eddie Arcaro:
When you start talking about great race riders, you begin with George Edward Arcaro. He could do anything on horseback that Jesse James, Tom Mix, Buffalo Bill, or the Lone Ranger could.

On Joby Arnold:
Joby Arnold is America's only woman handicapper of horses.
She picked the order of finish of the Derby one-two. But that's
nothing. She picked the order of finish of the day's second
race—a field of cunning platers who make a habit of outwitting
the bettors, which is not the toughest thing they have to do
in a day. Trainers who might not admit to me if one of their
horses had just broken two clocks or three legs, lose all their
reserve when Joby reins alongside and fastens those brown eyes
on them. They come across like a guy whose fingernails are
being pulled out with pliers.

On Chris McCarron:
Charles Dickens would have loved Chris McCarron. So would
Walt Disney. Eyes as blue as Galway Bay, framed by ringlets of
flame-red hair, he looked like a cross between Oliver Twist and
Bambi. Racing's Little Boy Blue.

On Lafitt Pincay Jr.:

Some guys ride horses like a Sioux warrior circling a wagon train, or a Cossack running down peasants. Others wheedle wins out of fainter-hearted horses. Pincay doesn't take any nonsense from a horse, but wins races the way Ruth hit homers. Horses seldom quite on Lafitt. Around the track, it is said they would jump over a cliff for him.

On Jenine Sahadi:

Well, Ms. Sahadi is a long way from being Madame Butterfly or riding to hounds. If you're looking for her any day soon, try the winner's circle at Hollywood Park. She has been there, holding the reins of a winner, more times than any trainer at the track. As of this weekend, a rousing 32 percent of her entries have won. That "J. Sahadi' you see in your program does not stand for "John" or "Joe" or "Jim."

On Willie Shoemaker:

Riding a racehorse is a little like playing a grand piano. You've got to have the touch of a concert artist. The only communication between horse and rider is through the hands and reins. . . . In short, when maestro Shoemaker sits down to play his horse, he gets the "Moonlight Sonata."

On Seattle Slew:

Slew was a compassionate horse. He never beat anybody more than he had to. He was like a poker player who lets you keep your watch and carfare home.

On Secretariat:

Now it's the week of the Belmont Stakes, and Secretariat, the horse, has been on the cover of *Time, Newsweek*, the *Blood Horse, Sports Illustrated*, and he looks like a $6 million steal. His stud book will be busier than a sultan's. If he loses the Belmont, he's going to take more money with him than a bank president absconding to Rio.

On Sunday Silence:

A horse they thought so little of they did everything but leave him on a park bench with a note on him: "Won the Kentucky Derby Saturday."

On Charlie Whittingham, veteran trainer:

Charlie Whittingham has been around horses so long he sleeps standing up.

On Winning Colors, a filly:

No female has ever won the Triple Crown. But, look at it this way: No colt is going to increase the male margin this year. And the way she won this one, there's no horse in the thing who knows what she looks like from the front. They wouldn't be able to recognize her on the street.

On racehorses, in general:

Two-year-old racehorses are like teenagers everywhere. All the good breeding in the world won't guarantee they won't, so to speak, run off with a rock band or join the circus or drop out generally and spend the rest of their lives breaking your heart. But, then, of course, some of them pay attention to business, join the establishment, make a name for themselves and succeed in business beyond your wildest expectations.

But it's not only the ones [athletes] who can read and write and even talk who get most of the pampering. That honor goes to a breed of sports heroes who don't have to answer telephones, reach decisions, hire agents or even feed themselves—thoroughbred racehorses. They are bona fide tantrum-throwing, breath-holding *enfants terribles* of the worst sort.

TENNIS

"Tennis is a game in which love counts nothing, deuces are wild, and the scoring system was invented by Lewis Carroll."

Tennis is a game in which love counts nothing, deuces are wild, and the scoring system was invented by Lewis Carroll. It's not a game, it's a multiplication table. . . . Six games win a set. But only if you stay two games ahead of your opponent. Why? You can win a baseball game by one run, a fight by one punch, a football game by one point. In soccer, that's about all you usually do score.

The game is as old as the pharaohs but it never really got out of the castles or the railroad barons' casinos in Newport. For thousands of years, everyone who played it wore or was white, and had a whole bunch of hyphens or Roman numerals in his name or was a baron or an earl. There wasn't a guy in it who didn't have two or more syllables in his first name. You couldn't understand him unless you went to Groton.

If you write about it for two weeks in a row, the truck drivers stop reading you. They can take only so much of a sport where a shutout is called love.

On Andre Agassi:

He doesn't run, he scurries. He hurries everywhere, always managing to look as if he were ten minutes late for an appointment or trying to catch a bus. His eyes dart all over the place, like a gambler with a low pair. He's ubiquitous on the court.

On Arthur Ashe:

Of all the athletes I have known, there was none whose intellect I had more respect for than Arthur Ashe's. You could get right down to the nitty-gritty of any subject with Arthur, and that included racial harmony—of which he was a passionate advocate.

On Boris Becker:

They used to say of Arnold Palmer that the only thing he did right with a golf club was win. Boris became the tennis equivalent. He hit off the wrong foot, his backhand was unclassic, his forehand collapsible—but the ball came rocketing back like one of Nolan Ryan's fastballs.

On Bjorn Borg:
He was far and away the best of his generation, maybe of any generation. He had an all-court game. He could slug, lob, play at the net, serve-and-volley, or kill you from the baseline.

On May Sutton Bundy:
What Thorpe was to track, Grange to football, or Ruth to baseball, May Sutton Bundy was to tennis. I felt as if I had spent an hour in another, better world.

On Michael Chang:
You can tell right away that Michael Chang isn't a tennis player. I mean, he doesn't grunt as if he were lifting a locomotive wheel when he hits a two-ounce ball full of air sixty feet. He doesn't throw rackets. He doesn't curse umpires, the crowd, line calls, ball boys, locker room attendants or post-match interviewers. He doesn't spit at the chair over a call. He doesn't come on court in a scraggly beard, his hair sticking out of the back of his cap like a horse's tail. And he doesn't cut his T-shirt so that his belly button shows on every shot.

On Jimmy Connors:
James Scott Connors is about as popular in the world of tennis
as a double fault.

On Stefan Edberg:
You can always tell Edberg because he wins. It's like getting
beat by the statue of Fred Perry they have outside Wimbledon.
It's hard to describe winning as boring. But Edberg makes a
case for it. No one will ever call him "Boom-Boom" or "the
Rocket" or "Big Stefan." If he gets a nickname, it will be
"Advantage Edberg."

On Chris Evert:
She played tennis with the automatic precision of a computer.
She hit these devastating winners from the baselines. Her face
was as impassive as a mug shot. She looked like something
you'd find on the lawn at the Dartmouth Winter Carnival. You
put on a sweater to talk to Chrissie Evert. She made a penguin
look hot and bothered. She looked as unattainable as Garbo, a
slope of Everest.

On Zina Garrison:

If Zina Garrison were a man, she'd probably be playing shortstop for the St. Louis Cardinals, scooping up ground balls in the hole, batting a .310 and stealing fifty to sixty bases. Or, she might be batting down passes in the Green Bay Packer secondary, or running back punts or starring on special teams. . . . But Zina is not a man. So she's scooping up ground strokes with a tennis racket instead of a glove, she's batting back serves and volleys, not curves, and the passes she intercepts are at the net.

On Steffi Graf:

She is as German as a glockenspiel. And fittingly, she plays this kind of Wagnerian game, full of crashing crescendos, heroic passages, lyric transitions. She attacks.

On Martina Hingis:

The first look you get at Martina Hingis, you don't know whether to buy her a lollipop or ask her to dance. I mean, you think this is Shirley Temple at the baseline and any minute she'll break into "On The Good Ship Lollipop." . . . For someone this young and this small to hit a ball this hard and this accurately shouldn't be legal. . . . Hingis is in command out there. She's as hard to discourage as an insurance salesman.

On John McEnroe:
If his tennis was a little ragged, his larynx was in Wimbledon form. He stood on the baseline with those cat's eyes of his, like a lion who sees a leaf moving in the bush across a clearing, and he whacked out opponents like Brad Gilbert while jawing with female fans, whom he called "lowlives."

On Martina Navratilova:
Martina Navratilova may very well be the most dominating there ever was in her sport. If she were a team, there'd be cries to break her up.

On Pete Sampras:
He's as American as the hot rod and probably could have been a cleanup hitter if someone hadn't put a racket in his hands at age seven. He plays tennis like a guy dealing blackjack. All he does is beat you.

On Monica Seles:
Monica has a two-handed forehand. But she backs it up with this full-voice grunt that she thinks makes her shot harder. It's for sure it makes it louder. You know Monica is on her game when center court sounds like feeding time at the zoo.

TRACK AND FIELD

"Nothing this side of Man o' War could challenge Carl Lewis in his heyday."

On Bob Beamon:

Bob Beamon was in the air just shorter than the Wright Brothers. . . . It wasn't a jump, it was an orbital flight.

On Gail Devers:

Devers knew well what real tragedy was, and it was not tripping over a hurdle. Tragedy was not losing a race, tragedy was losing your feet.

On Jackie Joyner-Kersee:

Jackie Joyner Kersee is not the best in the world in any one of the heptathlon's seven events, but she's the best in the world at all seven.

On Carl Lewis:

How do you measure athletic prowess? The guy who can hit harder, run faster or jump higher than anybody, right? Carl Lewis makes it on two out of three. And he never measured himself against the curve, the return of serve or the right cross. But when it came to running and jumping, well, nothing this side of Man o' War could challenge Carl Lewis in his heyday.

On Bob Mathias:

What Bob Mathias really was, was a one-man track team. He didn't have to do much about it. God and nature anticipated him. Whatever a mountain lion could do, Bob Mathias could do. He was brought up in the sunshine and breezes of the San Joaquin Valley, where vegetables and men grow in size to twice the national average.

On Edwin Moses:

I like to see Edwin Moses run the hurdles for the same reason I liked to see Rod Carew bat, Bing Crosby sing, Joe DiMaggio drift under a high fly, Joe Louis throw a left, Sammy Snead hit a drive, Swaps in the stretch, Palmer putt, Koufax with the hitter in a hole, Marcus Allen hit a line—or, for that matter, a Swiss make a watch, an Arab sell a rug, a Manolete fight a bull, or a Hemingway write about it, an Englishman do Shakespeare, or Roosevelt make a speech.

On Mary Decker Slaney:
In a sport practiced by a lot of women who look as if they should be running tugboats, Mary looks as if she just stepped off the runway at Givenchy's.

On Ruth Wysocki:
For one afternoon last June, she became the most famous Ruth since Babe. She beat the incomparable Decker, the Queen Mary of track and field, by sweeping past her in the stretch of the 1,500 with a dazzling 4:00.1, a clocking that lopped more than twelve seconds off her previous best and nipped Mary Decker by daylight.

Women's international track and field stars are beginning to look like someone you might call "Bubba." At a time when 90 percent of the adult female world wants to look like Bo Derek, they're working more towards looking like Bo Schembechler. In a world of "perfect 10s," they're "minus 3s."

DIFFERENT ARENAS

"Sports is just corporate America in cleats."

More Female Sports Figures

On Sharon Sites Adams, sailor:

Sharon Sites Adams crosses the Pacific traveling as light as a shark. Her only companions have fins on them. Even fish travel the ocean in schools. And it wasn't so long ago sailors were superstitious about having a woman on board. Sharon doesn't believe in having a woman on board either. Or men.

On Tai Babilonia, figure skater:

Put her on skates and in a tutu and Tai Babilonia looks like something out of a fairy tale or off the top of a music box. Tchaikovsky wrote ballets for people like this.

On Nadia Comaneci, gymnast:

Nadia Comaneci may make an "11" next time out on the uneven bars. She should break a leg to bring the competition down to her level. She is Peter Pan on a balance beam.

On Midge Dandridge, archer:

Midge Dandridge is the most menacing of all creatures—the silent killer. She is swift, sure, and deadly. A grizzly would probably bust out laughing if he saw her approach with her quiver full of arrows. She looks like a Valentine's Day card. But she makes Lizzie Borden look like a prankster.

On Anneli Drummond-Hay, equestrian:

Anneli Drummond-Hay is the most famous, fully dressed lady rider in British history. She can do more things on horseback than the James boys. She may be the best over hedges and rocks in female history. She's on horseback more than John Wayne.

On Margo Godfrey, surfer:

She took on more waves than the migrating gray whales. On the blips of the Scripps Oceanographic Institute, Margo Godfrey became as familiar a dot as the Coast Guard. Even the seals got to know her. She became as much of a part of the off-shore swell as kelp.

On Sonja He.,ie, figure skater:

Before Henie, it was hard to think of anything performed in a sequined costume to the strains of Rachmaninoff as sport. But Henie was one of the first to show that not all athletes had to have a ball or a stick in their hands to qualify.

On Shirley Muldowney, dragster:
Her hand-eye coordination is such that she probably could
have made a good living with the Dodgers if she were six
inches taller and forty pounds heavier.

On Judy Pachner, fisherman:
Judy can take a Nantucket sleigh ride with a twelve-pound
bass. She is under limit. She says she is five feet, but you know
how fishermen exaggerate. She says she weighs ninety pounds,
but that sounds like another fish story. The reason she's so suc-
cessful is the fish think she's one of them.

On Kathy Rude, racecar driver:
Kathy, who will wed race driver Ludwig Heimrath in October,
is going into the race for the same reason downed World War I
pilots went back up in their rickety Sopwith Camels. She's
testing herself for nerve and determination. The only thing
realistic about it is, the boys will be chasing her. After they get
a look at her with that helmet off, you can't blame them.

On Kristi Yamaguchi, figure skater:
On the ice she is the nearest thing to a living poem as an athlete
gets.

Sports is just corporate America in cleats. It should be listed on the Big Board. And it's the real opiate of the people.

On his birthday, in 1981:
I woke up Tuesday morning and went to look in the mirror. The guy in there was having a birthday, I won't tell you which one. Suffice it to say, he's much older than I.

On eating:
Babe Ruth, of course, was the all-time trencherman. His stomach used to rumble in the outfield if the other team had a big inning.

On heroes:
The public never forgives a guy who dents an idol, profanes an icon or shows up Santa Claus. You can kill all the buffalo, wipe out the cavalry, rob all the banks, sell the Statehouse, run rum, or join the Mafia—but don't mess around with America's sports idolatry. They don't forgive the guy who floored Dempsey, beat Willie Pep, ambushed Billy the Kid, hit more homers than Babe Ruth, shot more birdies than Hogan, or overtook Arnold Palmer.

On martial arts:
Just after you have been slammed to the ground in front of a
crowd, you are expected to stand at attention and bow gravely
to your opponent as if he had just handed you a plate of fortune cookies and tea.

On going into the Sportswriters Hall of Fame in 1978:
A Hall of Fame is something Ty Cobb belongs to. Red Grange.
Jim Brown. Ben Hogan. . . . But, what did I do—out-adjective
the next guy? Did I split fewer infinitives than anybody else?
Avoid hitting into the double negative? The pros talk about
"playing with pain." Did I write with pain, shrug off the hang-
overs better than anyone else and hit that space bar with desire?

On sportscaster Graham McNamee:
He didn't know much about sports. But he was a demon on
meteorology. He could do forty minutes on the changing of a
leaf color. It was said he went through an entire Rose Bowl
game without once alluding to the action on the field. The
snowcapped mountains, the Rose Queen, the floats, and the
movie stars were enough for Graham.

On colorful names:

When I was a kid back in Connecticut I used to love USC back-
fields. You had to be fascinated. I remember rolling the names off
my tongue. Morley Drury. Homer Griffith. Grenville Landsdell.
Gaius Shaver. Irvine Warburton. Orville Mohler. You read them
and felt like going out and throwing rocks at your mother and
father for naming you 'Jim' when they could have picked something romantic and sturdy like these lucky guys.

There have been lots of great names in baseball history. . . . but,
for sheer unadulterated alliteration, the all-time baseball name
belongs to Van Lingle Mungo. You can't even say it, you've got
to sing it. It sounds like something a guy would be singing from
the rigging of a banana boat coming into port, or like the
rumblings of a steel band. It's part calypso, part hog-call. The
consonants just tinkle along like a runaway calliope. Naturally,
Van Lingle Mungo is the only pitcher in the history of the game
whose name and fastball were both hummers.

On changing times:
The bulldozer is the worst invention of mankind—closely
followed by the amplifier.

On his being standoffish:
I like to keep people at arm's length because sooner or later
I'll probably have to bite 'em in the ass. Some still have the
teeth marks.

On Singin Smith, volleyball player:
Most people go up in the air like human pile drivers and
attempt to smash the ball into the core of the earth so deep
under the shoreline that colonies of sea life come to the surface
and it takes two strong men to excavate it. Singin Smith prefers
to go up in the air, hang there like a hummingbird while he
sizes up the defensive tendencies of the opponents, then dunk
the ball softly in a corner of the court he sees they have left
unprotected.

On Karch Kiraly, volleyball player:
If he were in basketball, they'd call him "Magic." In baseball, he'd be "the Man" or maybe even "the Thumper." In tennis, he might be "Boom Boom." In golf, maybe "the Hawk." He'd probably have a shoe contract like Air Jordan—except his sport doesn't wear shoes. Like Lawrence of Arabia, his domain is the burning sand. He has been in more sand than a camel.

On Irving Crane, pool player:
I guess the animals in nature with the greatest protective coloration are (1) the zebra; (2) the leopard; (3) the salamander, and (4) Irving Crane. Irving Crane is a pool player, probably the world's best, and pool players are like spies—the less conspicuous they are, the better.

On Senator Robert Kennedy's assassination in 1968:
Bobby Kennedy is going home on the Pennsylvania Central. No change of trains. His ticket is punched clear through. No charge for the man in the last car, Conductor. He has paid his way to Arlington.

RFK loved sports. Some men sample wine of the country they visit. He sampled the danger. Where they had the sea, he surfed. Or sailed. Where they had mountains, he climbed. Where they had rivers, he forded. He lived on the rapids of life. He reached for summits, not safety. You found him on a boat, a board, a ski, a field, a horse, a bench, a base. He opted for adventure. He played, and he watched.

On rodeos:

Not since the Christians and the lions has there been an athletic contest quite like the rodeo. Wild animals versus unarmed men. These are the last of the *High Noon* characters. An arena full of Gary Coopers. The modern versions of Wyatt Earp.

Have you ever seen a Brahma bull up close? When their hind hooves are high in the air and you can see their entire underbelly trembling with uncontrolled rage, their tiny demented eyes rolling malevolently in their massive heads, their mouths flecked with rabid foam, it's like looking into one of the inner circles of hell. Eight seconds can seem like a year in an interrogation cell in the Lubyanka.

On bull rider Wacey Cathey:

If someone saw Wacey in a lawyer's office on Park Avenue, he would take him for a junior partner of the firm. If they told him he rode Brahma bulls for a living, he would edge away from them. Wacey doesn't look as if he could get onto anything more ferocious than a BMW. . . . He rides the bull like a commuter. Even to the bull, he looks like one.

On Charles Sampson, African-American bull rider:

Although the Old West was full of black cowboys, Charles Sampson is a pioneer of the mold of a Jackie Robinson in this sport. But it's a distinction that, although it doesn't bore him, doesn't seem to him to have much relevance. "Bulls aren't prejudiced," he says. "They hate everybody, regardless of race, creed or color."

Every year at this time I go to the Shriners Crippled Children's Hospital. Every year, I hope there will be no one there. But it's never to be so. There are sixty beds and sixty wheel carts and 120 crutches and they're all filled. Heartbreak is playing to capacity. Human suffering has the S.R.O. sign out. Misery never sleeps.

⌒

On Sports Illustrated:

It's impossible to downplay the importance of the magazine on the incredible explosion in sports in the last half of the twentieth century. Consider that one player, the great Joe DiMaggio, was paid as much as $100,000 in that benighted era. Today, high school kids make more than any Rockefeller then.

Sports Illustrated came out in the era and the aura of television, the great Aztec god of games . . . some of us were leery of the challenge. TV already had begun to bring down the cash cow of the company, *Life*, whose still pictures couldn't compete with TV's moving, talking pictures.

⌒

On Humphrey Bogart:

He always played tough guys but he was anything but . . . after two drinks, he thinks he's Bogart.

On Billy Crystal:

He's the only guy in the world sorry he didn't make it big in baseball. The rest of us are glad of it. Because Billy Crystal is one of the foremost makes-you-feel-good entertainers of our day. His name on a marquee insures a film's success. He could have been one of the [baseball] greats. Made the world forget Nellie Fox. Hit the Mazeroski home run. We could have had handy headlines. "Red Sox 'Crystal-ized' by Billy Bat!"

On Kevin Costner's bankability:

Bankers would bankroll Costner doing grand opera if he wanted.

MURRAY'S LAWS

Nothing is ever so bad it can't be made worse by firing the coach.

A free agent is anything but.

If you smile when everything about you is going wrong, join the San Francisco 49ers.

Things always get worse just before they get impossible.

Nothing is ever accomplished by reason—look at Woody Hayes.

You can fool all of the people all of the time—if you own the network.

The "Peter Principle" that everything keeps rising until it reaches its level of incompetence is best illustrated by the Minnesota Vikings in the Super Bowl.

Anger is always a proper substitute for logic.

If everything else fails, throw it away.

The old Army game: "If it moves, salute it, if it doesn't move, it must be the Rams and Atlanta."

Whatever can go to New York, will. Whatever can't will go to Philadelphia.

The wrong Ram quarterback is the one that's in there.

Any two TV programs you like will go on opposite each other.

Hockey is a game played by six good skaters and the home team.

I'm consistent; you're stubborn.

Rhetoric is the art of being wrong out loud.

You're taking yourself too seriously in the company when you forget it's not your money.

Money isn't everything; look at the California Angels.

When you think everything is hopeless, just remember Yogi Berra.

Cars with the lucky pieces hanging off the rearview mirror will always seem to star in bad accidents.

The guy with the coat slung over his shoulder without his arms in the sleeves in movies is up to no good.

Never tape anything but your mouth.

The race is not always to the swift. Look at Jack Nicklaus.

Never envy the big star of the show. That turkey you're eating thought he had a no-cut contract.

JIM VS. METROPOLIS

On Spokane:

The only trouble with Spokane, Washington, as a city is that there's nothing to do after ten o'clock. In the morning.

On Cincinnati:

You have to think that when Dan'l Boone was fighting the Indians for this territory, he didn't have Cincinnati in mind for it. . . . If Cincinnati were human, they'd bury it.

On Palm Springs, the self-proclaimed golf capitol of the world:
Palm Springs is an inland sandbar man has wrestled from the rodents and the Indians to provide a day camp for the over-privileged adults.

On St. Louis:

The city had a bond issue recently and the local papers campaigned for it on a slogan, "Progress or Decay," and decay won in a landslide.

On Los Angeles:

It's four hundred miles of slide area. One minute you're spreading a picnic lunch on a table at the Palisades and the next minute you're treading water in the Pacific. It's a place that has a dry river but a hundred thousand swimming pools.

On New York:
(It's) the largest chewing gum receptacle in the world.

On Philadelphia:
Philadelphia was founded in 1776 and has been going downhill ever since.

On Pittsburgh:
(It's) America's night light, a city that gave us ten thousand bowling shirts with Tic-Toc Grill across the back.

On San Francisco:
It fancies itself Camelot, but comes off more like Cleveland. Its legacy to the world is the quiche.

On the Twin Cities:
Minneapolis and Saint Paul don't like each other very much, and from what I could see I don't blame either of them.

AND THEY SAID

"My morning coffee will never be the same without Jim Murray's column."

On Murray's being selected for the Baseball Hall of Fame:
JIM, YOU ARE WITHOUT A DOUBT, ONE OF THE FINEST WRITERS IN THIS COUNTRY AND YOUR INDUCTION INTO THE HALL OF FAME IS SO DESERVING. . . . I'M PROUD TO KNOW YOU.

—*Tommy Lasorda*

HE COULD WRITE ABOUT ANYTHING, BUT THE BEST THING HE DID WAS TELL STORIES ABOUT THE PEOPLE WHO MADE SPORTS WHAT IT IS. CAN THERE BE A MORE FITTING COMBINATION THAN ONE OF THE BEST SPORTSWRITERS OF OUR TIME WRITING ABOUT SOME OF THE BEST OF SPORTS PERSONALITIES HE COVERED? JIM IS GONE NOW, BUT THE LIBRARY HE LEFT BEHIND REMAINS.

—*Arnold Palmer*

JIM MURRAY WAS THE "BEST OF THE BEST"! JIM MURRAY THE WRITER WAS JIM MURRAY THE MAN—CLEVER, HUMOROUS, UNBELIEVABLY KNOWLEDGEABLE, INSIGHTFUL, AND CARING. HOW PROUD I WILL ALWAYS BE TO HAVE CALLED HIM MY FRIEND.

—*Jack Nicklaus*

TO HAVE JIM WRITE ABOUT YOU, THAT FELT AS GREAT AS HAVING YOUR NAME ENGRAVED ON A TROPHY.

—*Jeff Sluman*

SO FAR I HAVE RECEIVED TWENTY-EIGHT COPIES OF YOUR ARTICLE
ABOUT ME AND THE SENIOR PGA TOUR. THE ARTICLE WAS TERRIFIC;
YOU MADE ME SOUND BETTER THAN I AM.

—*Jim Colbert*

YOUR STORY OF MY TEN-YEAR ANNIVERSARY WAS JUST SUPER! THANK
YOU FOR TAKING TIME OUT OF YOUR BUSY SCHEDULE FOR ME!

—*Mary Lou Retton-Kelley*

*U.S. Women's Open champion Meg Mallon's response when asked which
three people from history she would like to have dinner with:*
BABE DIDRIKSON—I READ ALL OF HER BOOKS WHEN I WAS A CHILD;
MOTHER TERESA, THE MOST UNSELFISH AND GIVING PERSON IN
HISTORY; AND LOU GEHRIG, A KINDHEARTED MAN WHO FACED
ADVERSITY ON AND OFF THE FIELD WITH STYLE AND CLASS. IF I
COULD INVITE A FOURTH, IT WOULD BE JIM MURRAY, THE PULITZER
PRIZE-WINNING SPORTSWRITER. HE'D BE ABLE TO CAPTURE THE
MOMENT ON PAPER.

IT ALWAYS HAS BEEN AND STILL IS A JOY TO READ MURRAY, WHO
NEVER STRIKES OUT AND IS NOT *A* PRIZE—BUT *THE* PRIZE—OF OUR
PROFESSION.

—*Shirley Povich*, Washington Post, *1997*

YOU DO THE *LOS ANGELES TIMES* PROUD YEAR AFTER YEAR WITH
OR WITHOUT BEING NAMED TOP SPORTSWRITER BY YOUR PEERS,
BUT THIRTEEN WINS IS RATHER PHENOMENAL.

> —*Otis Chandler, publisher,* Los Angeles Times, *1978*

THE LIFETIME ACHIEVEMENT AWARD DEFINES THE BEST OF OUR
JOURNALISM, AND THIS IS DEFINITELY JIM MURRAY. FOR THIRTY-
SEVEN YEARS, HE HAS DELIGHTED, EDUCATED, AMUSED, AND
OUTRAGED READERS IN THE *TIMES*. THE LIGHTNESS OF HIS
WRITING BELIES THE DEPTH OF HIS THOUGHT. HE WRITES ABOUT
SPORTS, YES, BUT HE IS REALLY WRITING ABOUT LIFE.

> —*Michael Parks, editor,* Los Angeles Times, *on Murray's
> receiving the Lifetime Achievement Award from the* Times, *1998*

TO PARAPHRASE ONE OF HIS OWN LINES, JIM MURRAY IS A
NATIONAL INSTITUTION. THEY SHOULD HANG A COLLECTION OF
HIS COLUMNS IN THE SMITHSONIAN. THE PROBLEM WOULD BE
PICKING OUT THE BEST ONES. LIKE, WHICH OF REMBRANDT'S
WORKS DO YOU CHOSE?

> —*Woody Woodburn, the* Daily Breeze, *Torrance, California*

FOR REASONS FOREVER A MYSTERY, MURRAY PRACTICALLY ADOPTED ME WHEN I MET HIM AT MY FIRST WORLD SERIES, BETWEEN LOS ANGELES AND MINNESOTA IN 1965. HE TOOK ME EVERYWHERE, INTRODUCED ME TO EVERYONE. I FELT LIKE AN ART STUDENT PERCHED ON MICHELANGELO'S PALETTE.

—*Edwin Pope*, Miami Herald

I'D SAY WITHIN THE BUSINESS, JIM WAS A LEGEND TO EVERYBODY EXCEPT HIMSELF. I HAVE KNOWN HIM FOR THIRTY-FIVE YEARS, I GUESS, AND HE WAS A WONDERFUL FRIEND. ALSO, THE TOUGHEST S.O.B. I'VE EVER KNOWN.

—*Blackie Sherrod*, Dallas Morning News

JIM WAS MORE THAN A SPORTSWRITER. HE PRODUCED LITERATURE. NO ONE IN SPORTS JOURNALISM WAS MORE REVERED OR MORE SHABBILY IMITATED.

—*Furman Bisher*, Atlanta Journal-Constitution

HE JUST EMBARRASSED US ALL BECAUSE HE HAD THAT GIFT. AND HE WAS AS GIFTED OUT OF THE PRESS BOX AS HE WAS ON DEADLINE. FOR THE YOUNGER GUYS IN THE BUSINESS, WE WANTED TO BE IN AWE OF HIM, BUT HE WOULDN'T LET US.

—*Bob Verdi*, Chicago Tribune/Golf Digest

A Hall of Fame sports columnist, at the Super Bowl. (File photo courtesy of Linda McCoy-Murray)

HE NEVER DID COMPLAIN. HE NEVER HAD THE TIME, WHAT WITH ASKING HOW YOU WERE DOING. IT DIDN'T MATTER IF YOU WERE THE THIRD-STRING TENNIS WRITER FOR THE *MODESTO NEWS*, WHEN YOU LEFT MURRAY YOU WERE NEVER QUITE SURE WHICH ONE OF YOU WAS THE LEGEND.

—*Rick Reilly*, Sports Illustrated

MURRAY LOVED WRITING ABOUT GOLF, BUT HE JOKED THAT HE COULDN'T DEVOTE TOO MANY COLUMNS TO IT. "I'LL LOSE THE TRUCK DRIVERS," HE SAID. IN ALL THOSE YEARS OF WRITING ALL HIS ELEGANT, FUNNY, THOUGHTFUL COLUMNS, MURRAY NEVER LOST ANYBODY.

—*Thomas Bonk*, Los Angeles Times

IN THE 1960S, THE RAMS WERE IN BALTIMORE TO PLAY THE COLTS. ON THE EVE OF THE GAME, MURRAY, RAM PUBLICIST JACK TEELE, AND I GOT INTO A CAB TO GO OUT TO DINNER AT A FAMOUS BALTIMORE RESTAURANT. AFTER WEAVING THROUGH THE STREETS FOR ALMOST AN HOUR, MURRAY TOLD THE LOST CABDRIVER, "CABBIE, TAKE US TO A CAB."

—*Mal Florence*, Los Angeles Times

DAMN, THAT GUY WAS GOOD. AND NOT A JERK ABOUT IT. JIM WAS
AS IMPRESSED WITH HIS OWN WRITING AS HE WAS WITH THE
NIGHTLIFE IN MINNEAPOLIS. IT WAS A PLEASURE—AND HONOR
FOR ME—TO SIT NEXT TO HIM IN A PRESS BOX.

—*Scott Ostler*, San Francisco Chronicle

ONLY JIM, OF ALL THE GREAT SPORTSWRITERS, ALWAYS GOT IT
RIGHT AND ALWAYS GOT IT FUNNY.

—*Dave Kindred*, The Sporting News

JIM MURRAY IS NOT MERELY A GREAT SPORTSWRITER. HE IS A
GREAT AMERICAN WRITER WHO DESERVES TO BE THOUGHT OF
WITH MARK TWAIN, ERNEST HEMINGWAY AND JOHN UPDIKE AS
WELL AS RED SMITH AND JIMMY CANNON.

—*Dave Anderson, fellow Pulitzer Prize winner*, New York Times

MY MORNING COFFEE WILL NEVER BE THE SAME WITHOUT JIM
MURRAY'S COLUMN. HE WAS A BRILLIANT OBSERVER, WHO ALWAYS
WATCHED WITH HIS HEART.

—*Merv Griffin*

*A scintillating sextet of sportswriters: (left to right) Blackie Sherrod,
Jim Murray, Edwin Pope, Furman Bisher, Dave Kindred,
and Bill Millsaps.(Photo courtesy of Linda McCoy-Murray)*

I HAVE SO MUCH RESPECT FOR A WORDSMITH. JIM MURRAY WAS ONE I READ SLOWLY, SAVORING EVERY WORD. I ALWAYS READ HIS WORDS WITH A MIXTURE OF ENVY AND ADMIRATION—WISHING THAT I HAD HALF THE COMMAND OF LANGUAGE AND THOUGHTFUL WAY OF MAKING A POINT THAT HE DID. I MET JIM IN THE SIXTIES. WHENEVER HE WOULD INTERVIEW ME, I WOULD WORRY A LITTLE BIT. NOT THAT HE WAS UNFAIR, BUT BECAUSE HE WAS SO ENTERTAINING AT ANOTHER'S EXPENSE. SO I WASN'T USUALLY TOO THRILLED TO BE HIS SUBJECT; IT'S MUCH MORE ENJOYABLE WHEN THE FOCUS IS ON SOMEBODY ELSE.

—Mario Andretti

AMONG HIS FRIENDS IN THE SPORTSWRITING BUSINESS, JIM WAS A MAN WE ENJOYED AND ADMIRED IN EQUAL PROPORTIONS. GIFTED AS HE WAS AT DISCUSSING THE TRIUMPHS OF OTHERS, IT'S DOUBTFUL THAT ANY ATHLETE HE WROTE ABOUT ACHIEVED AS MUCH GREATNESS AGAINST ADVERSITY AS HE DID.

—Dan Foster

MAYBE AN ENGLISH PROFESSOR WOULD NEGLECT TO TELL YOU, BUT GOOD WRITING IS FUN. IT CAN BE AN ESSENCE IN LIFE'S MERRIMENT. SOLEMNITY WAS INVARIABLY A STRANGER IN THE WORDS OF JIM MURRAY.

—Don Freeman, San Diego Union-Tribune

IT ISN'T EASY TRYING TO BE LOU GEHRIG WHEN THEY MAKE YOU BAT BEHIND BABE RUTH. WITH HIS ONE GOOD EYE, JIM MURRAY JUST KEEPS KNOCKING 'EM OUT OF THE PARK. HE SEES MORE CLEARLY THAN ANYBODY I KNOW. "KING OF THE SPORTS PAGE" IS WHAT *SPORTS ILLUSTRATED* CALLED HIM, AND THAT'S WHAT HE IS, THE SULTAN OF THOUGHT.

—*Mike Downey, former columnist,* Los Angeles Times

JIM BROUGHT A PERSPECTIVE TO HIS WORK THAT MOST OF US TRYING TO WORK THE SAME BEAT CAN'T, PROVIDING A REMINDER THAT THERE WAS A DORIS DAY BEFORE THERE WAS A DEMI MOORE, AN ELGIN BAYLOR BEFORE MAGIC JOHNSON, AN ART ARAGON BEFORE AN OSCAR DE LA HOYA, A BOB WATERFIELD BEFORE A JOHN ELWAY.

—*Randy Harvey,* Los Angeles Times

PART OF MY WORK WITH MURRAY WAS TO READ TO HIM. MOST MORNINGS HE WANTED TO KNOW HOW PETE ROSE DID. MURRAY WAS A GREAT FAN OF ROSE. JIM ONCE SAID, "YOU ASK PETE A QUESTION AND THEN STAND BACK."

—*John Sheibe,* Los Angeles Times, *who for the last six months of 1979 drove Murray during a temporary loss of eyesight due to a detached retina*

WHAT SOMETIMES AGGRAVATED ME ABOUT JIM WAS THAT HE
COULDN'T SEEM TO UNDERSTAND WHY THE REST OF US LABORED
OVER OUR WRITING. HE THOUGHT EVERYBODY COULD BE JIM
MURRAY—THAT IT WAS NO BIG DEAL. I'VE NEVER KNOWN
ANYONE SO GIFTED WHO TOOK HIMSELF LESS SERIOUSLY. NO ONE
COULD WRITE THE WAY HE COULD, YET HE WAS AN EVEN BETTER
PERSON THAN A COLUMNIST.

—*Skip Bayless*, San Jose Mercury News

HIS STYLE WAS PERSONAL, AND HIS METAPHORS AND SIMILES
WERE SO OUTSIZED THAT THEY DIDN'T WORK FOR MOST PEOPLE.
HE WAS AN EXAMPLE OF ARTISTRY SO UNIQUE THAT IT'S NOT
WELL IMITATED. TO BE ABLE TO SIT THERE DECADE AFTER DECADE
AND PILE REFERENCES ON TOP OF EACH OTHER LIKE HE DID IS
AMAZING. . . . THE FIRST THING I HEARD ABOUT HIM WAS HOW
INCREDIBLY UNPRETENTIOUS HE WAS. YOU'D SEE HIM AT BIG
EVENTS, BUT HE WAS A LURKER, NOT A BOMBASTIC PRESENCE.
YOU'D SEE HIM WITH HIS QUIET MODUS OPERANDI, AND THEN HE
WOULD COME OUT WITH THESE VICIOUS CITY RIPS, AND IT WAS
HARD TO BELIEVE THEY WERE COMING FROM THIS SAME GUY,
WHO WAS KIND OF MOUSY IN PERSON.

—*Bob Ryan*, Boston Globe

READING JIM WAS ALWAYS A TREAT, BUT KNOWING HIM WAS
REALLY FUN—EVEN THOUGH I DON'T KNOW WHOSE SNORING
WAS MORE INVASIVE WHEN WE ROOMED TOGETHER AT THE
POLAND SPRING INN FOR THE SECOND ALI-LISTON FIGHT.

—*Bud Collins*, Boston Globe

HE MADE HIS READERS LAUGH AND CRY, ALL THE WHILE PEPPERING
THEM WITH ENOUGH ONE-LINERS TO LAND YOU A WEEK AT THE
PALACE. HE LEVELED CITIES WITH TONGUE-IN-CHEEK DESCRIPTIONS,
HUMANIZED BY HYPERBOLE AND PUNCTURED THE POMPOUS WITH
HIS LITERARY LANCE. EVERY DAY HE FACED THE SAME CHALLENGE,
THE SAME BLANK PIECE OF PAPER TAUNTINGLY UNFURLED AND
HANGING OUT OF THE TYPEWRITER LIKE A MOCKING TONGUE,
DARING HIM TO BE DIFFERENT, FRESH, FUNNY, AND INCISIVE. AND
EVERY DAY FOR MORE THAN THIRTY-FIVE YEARS, JIM MURRAY NOT
ONLY ACCEPTED THAT CHALLENGE BUT TRIUMPHED.

—*Vin Scully*

DO YOU KNOW THE WAY CERTAIN THINGS JUST GET BURNED INTO YOUR BRAIN AND THEY NEVER LEAVE? IN THE MID-SIXTIES, IN HIGH SCHOOL HERE, I PICKED UP A JIM MURRAY COLUMN AND HE WAS IN CINCINNATI, AND IT WAS THAT FAMOUS LINE WHERE HE WAS AT CROSLEY FIELD AND THE FREEWAY, I-75, WAS BEING CONSTRUCTED OUTSIDE THE BALLPARK. AND HE HAD BEEN GOING THERE FOR YEARS, AND THEY HAD COMPLETED ABOUT NINE MORE FEET. AND JIM WROTE, "IT MUST BE KENTUCKY'S TURN TO USE THE CEMENT MIXER."

SO IN 1971, I AM OFFERED THE JOB AS THE BROADCASTER FOR THE CINCINNATI REDS. THIS IS A DREAM COME TRUE AND I CAN'T BELIEVE IT, AND I GO TO CINCINNATI AND MEET WITH THE GENERAL MANAGER OF THE TEAM, AND HE CALLS ME UP AND HE SAYS, "AL, WE'RE HONORED TO ASK YOU TO BECOME THE NUMBER ONE BROADCASTER FOR THE CINCINNATI REDS." AND, I SWEAR TO YOU, ALL I CAN THINK OF SAYING, THOUGH I DIDN'T, WAS, "WHERE IS THE CEMENT MIXER?"

—*Al Michaels*

THERE'S AN OLD ADAGE USED ABOUT SPORTS THAT "RECORDS ARE MADE TO BE BROKEN." AND I THINK IN ALMOST EVERY INSTANCE, THEY ARE. BUT I'LL TELL YOU ONE THING, THE RECORDS OF JIM MURRAY'S WRITINGS WILL NEVER BE EQUALED, LET ALONE SURPASSED.

—*Chick Hearn*

Excerpts from Celebrity Letters to Jim:

THANK YOU FOR EVERYTHING YOU HAVE DONE FOR US. MAY EVERY DAY OF THE NEW YEAR ABOUND IN LIFE'S TREASURES FOR YOU.

—Lucy and Desi Arnaz, December 24, 1952

A HUNDRED THOUSAND ROSES COULDN'T HAVE BEEN SWEETER THAN *TIME* MAGAZINE WAS TO ME THIS WEEK. THANK YOU SO MUCH, LOVE.

—Rosemary Clooney, February 19, 1953

I APPRECIATED, MORE THAN ANY OTHER ASPECTS OF THE EXPERI-ENCE, TWO THINGS; ONE OF WHICH IS THE NEW PERSPECTIVE HE LENT ME OF MYSELF IN RELATION TO THE WORLD ABOUT ME AND SECONDLY IS YOUR HAVING BEEN AS HONEST AND DEVOTEDLY THOROUGH AS YOU WERE. MOST OF ALL I THINK THAT IT WAS YOUR LACK OF PRECONCEPTION AND YOUR INSISTENT OPENNESS OF MIND THAT MADE IT THE MOST PLEASANT EXPERIENCE WITH THE PRESS TO DATE.

—Marlon Brando

LOTS OF FELLOWS GET PAID FOR DOING THIS KIND OF WORK, BUT LOTS OF FELLOWS DON'T PUT IN THE CARE AND EFFORT THAT YOU DO YOURS.

—*John Wayne, February 28, 1952*

I USED TO HATE TO GET UP IN THE MORNING. THERE SEEMED TO BE NOTHING WORTH LOOKING FORWARD TO. THIS HAS ALL BEEN CHANGED SINCE YOU ARRIVED ON THE *L.A. TIMES.* NOW I LEAP OUT OF MY WIFE'S BED AND RUSH FOR YOUR COLUMN. THIS IS QUITE A TRIBUTE TO YOUR LITERARY PROWESS, FOR MY WIFE HAPPENS TO BE A VERY BEAUTIFUL WOMAN.

—*Groucho Marx, March 17, 1961*

I HAVE NEVER WRITTEN A FAN LETTER TO A COLUMNIST—OF ANY KIND. BUT THIS IS REALLY MORE THAN A FAN LETTER—IT IS A THANK YOU FOR TWO OF THE MOST SINCERE AND BEAUTIFULLY WRITTEN ARTICLES ON EVENTS OF OUR TIME. THE WORDS POURED FROM YOUR HEART RIGHT INTO MINE.

—*Marlo Thomas, June 14, 1968*

I'M STILL ENJOYING YOUR DAILY COLUMNS. YOU CERTAINLY HAVE COMPILED A MONUMENTAL LIBRARY OF HUMOROUS AND SERIOUS WRITINGS. HOPE YOU FLOURISH.

—Bing Crosby, March 27, 1974

I KNOW WRITING, THOUGH. AND WHAT THIS NOTE'S ABOUT: MAYBE A YEAR AND A HALF AGO WHEN I'D JUST FINISHED *ROOTS* AND MOVED HERE, I BEGAN READING YOUR WORK NOW OR THEN IN THE *TIMES*. THE MORE I DID, THE MORE I PERCEIVED—THIS GUY IS DAMNED GOOD! AND FOR A LONG TIME I'VE JUST HAD IT IN MIND TO TELL YOU THAT. YOU ARE ONE FINE WRITER, MY FRIEND!

—Alex Haley, August 14, 1977

WHEN I GOT BACK FROM JAPAN AND HONOLULU, THEY SHOWED ME YOUR COLUMN OF JULY 4, 1985, AND I WANT TO THANK YOU VERY MUCH. I'M HAVING WALLPAPER MADE OUT OF IT SO I CAN KISS IT EVERYDAY. I DON'T KNOW HOW TO REALLY THANK YOU. IF I WAS A GIRL I COULD THINK OF SOMETHING, BUT SINCE I'M JUST A HACKER, I OFFER YOU TWO ASIDE AT LAKESIDE FOR A NICKEL ANY DAY.

—Bob Hope, July 16, 1985

I'VE BEEN A WEAK-KNEED FAN OF YOURS FOR YEARS; EVEN
HAVING YOU TO DINNER AT MY HOUSE DID NOTHING TO LESSEN
THE PASSION OF MY ADMIRATION. BUT TODAY'S COLUMN IS
PERHAPS THE FUNNIEST PIECE OF WRITING I'VE READ ANYWHERE,
LET ALONE IN THE SPORTS SECTION. YOUR GENIUS IS UNDENIABLE,
AND I LOOK FORWARD TO SEEING YOU IN PERSON SOON.

—*William Shatner, July 3, 1997*

I ENTHUSIASTICALLY ENDORSE YOUR NOMINATION OF STEFFI GRAF
AS SPORTSMAN OF THE YEAR. HER DOMINATION OF WOMEN'S
TENNIS IS UNDENIABLE AND OVERWHELMING. HER BLAZING GIFTS
AS A PLAYER, AS WELL AS HER UNVARYING SPORTSMANSHIP, MAKE
HER AN IRRESISTIBLE CHOICE. IF *SPORTS ILLUSTRATED* PICKS HER,
THEY WILL ALSO MAKE A SIGNIFICANT STATEMENT FOR WOMEN
ATHLETES. WHO DO I WRITE AT *SI*?

—*Charlton Heston, December 14, 1989*

President Gerald Ford and Jim Murray
(File photo courtesy of Linda McCoy-Murray)

ON MURRAY'S WINNING THE PULITZER PRIZE IN 1990

I'M OLD ENOUGH TO HAVE READ THE BEST OF ARTHUR DALEY, RED SMITH, AND DAVE ANDERSON, BUT THE JIM MURRAY WORK IS AT THE "HEAD OF THE CLASS."

—Gerald Ford

WHEN SOMEONE HAS BROUGHT AS MUCH JOY AND ENLIGHTEN- MENT TO OTHERS AS YOU HAVE, HE SURE AS HELL DESERVES SOMETHING TERRIFIC IN RETURN.

—Jack Lemmon

LET ME ADD MY NAME TO THE LONG LIST OF THOSE OFFERING SINCEREST CONGRATULATIONS ON YOUR LATEST AND MOST DESERVED HONOR. NOT MANY GUYS HAVE A SPINK AND A PULITZER AND YOU CERTAINLY DESERVE BOTH.

—Jack Lang, executive secretary,
Baseball Writers' Association of America

I'M GLAD YOUR EXCELLENT SPORTSWRITING HAS BEEN
RECOGNIZED, BECAUSE I'VE ALWAYS CONSIDERED YOU ONE OF
THE FAIREST, MOST KNOWLEDGEABLE WRITERS AROUND.

—Pete Rose

CONGRATULATIONS. IT'S ABOUT TIME!

—Gene Kelly

WE ARE THRILLED BUT NOT SURPRISED.

—Gloria and Jimmy Stewart

YOU HAVE A TRUE GIFT FOR WRITING IN A WAY THAT MAKES ALL
SPORTS FANS LOOK FORWARD TO THE MORNING PAPER. YOUR
WRITING ENRICHES OUR LIVES AND I AM PROUD TO BE AMONG
YOUR MANY FANS.

—Ronald Reagan

IT'S ABOUT TIME THE PRIZE COMMITTEE CAME TO THEIR SENSES
AND GAVE THE PRIZE TO THE ONE MAN WHO COULD RETIRE THE
TROPHY IF HE WANTED TO.

—*George F. Will*

CONGRATULATIONS ON RECEIVING THE NOBEL PRIZE FOR SPORTS
COMMENTARY.

—*Gene Autry*

IF I WROTE YOU A CONGRATULATORY LETTER EVERY TIME I THINK
YOU DESERVE ONE YOU'D BE HEARING FROM ME EVERY DAY. RE:
THE PULITZER PRIZE—APPLAUSE, APPLAUSE, APPLAUSE!

—*Steve Allen*

DAY AFTER DAY, YOUR ABILITY TO INTELLECTUALLY, HUMOROUSLY
AND REALISTICALLY EXAMINE THE WORLD OF SPORTS THROUGH
YOUR MICROSCOPIC EYES, HAS PROVED TO BE AS IMPORTANT TO
ME (AND COUNTLESS READERS) AS MY ORANGE JUICE, COFFEE
AND CEREAL.

—*Monty Hall*

Gene Autry and Jim Murray.
(Marc Glassman photo courtesy of Linda McCoy-Murray)

FOR A MAN THAT GIVES SO MUCH PLEASURE TO OTHERS, THIS IS A WELL-DESERVED RECOGNITION.

—Kirk Douglas

RED SMITH AND JIM MURRAY. THOSE TWO WINNERS ALONE KEEP THE PULITZER AT THE FRONT OF THE PACK.

—Tom Brokaw

FOR ALL OF US WHO ARE YOUR FANS, YOU WON THIS PRIZE YEARS AGO AND MANY TIMES, BUT IT IS NICE TO SEE "THEM" MAKE IT OFFICIAL.

—Jack Whitaker

JUDGE CRATER IS FOUND. ROY RIEGELS RAN THE RIGHT WAY. JIM MURRAY HAS WON THE PULITZER PRIZE.

—Tom Callahan

I ALWAYS SAID YOU'D BE A SUCCESS ONE DAY. I AM PLEASED AND PROUD TO HAVE SERVED WITH YOU. DID YOU GET THE PRIZE FOR YOUR FUNNIEST LINES—YOUR EXPENSE ACCOUNTS?

—*Bill Shirley, former sports editor*, Los Angeles Times

THEY FINALLY GOT TASTE. I'M HONORED TO CALL YOU MY FRIEND. YOU ARE ONE OF THE PEOPLE WHO HAS ALWAYS MADE ME PROUD TO DO THIS WORK.

—*Mike Lupica*

HOW MANY INDY 500 WINS DOES IT TAKE TO EQUAL A PULITZER? MY BEST WISHES AND HEARTIEST CONGRATULATIONS ON THIS GREAT HONOR.

—*Danny Sullivan*

MY BROTHER, JOHN, IS A REPORTER FOR THE *NEW YORK TIMES* AND HE TOLD ME YEARS AGO HOW PROUD HIS *TIMES* COLLEAGUES WERE THAT THEIR PAPER HAD A MONOPOLY ON PULITZER PRIZE WINNERS IN SPORTS. WELL, THAT MONOPOLY WAS BROKEN WHEN YOU SO DESERVEDLY WERE AWARDED A PULITZER LAST MONTH.

—*Paul Tagliabue*

ON THE PULITZER PRIZE, IN HIS OWN WORDS

I'm perfectly astonished at getting a Pulitzer Prize. Joseph Pulitzer and Horace Greeley must be spinning in their graves. I always thought you had to bring down a government to win this. All I ever did was quote Tommy Lasorda accurately.

One of the nicest things about the Pulitzer was the elation of my friends. Frankly, that was my Pulitzer and I'm grateful to the Pulitzer Committee for making it possible to hear from so many old pals and to share the honor with them.

This is going to make it a little easier on the guy who writes my obit!